Dementia Diary

A love story to the end

D1274082

Ali Sinclair

Dementia Diary: A love story to the end

© 2020 Ali Sinclair

ISBN 978-1-9163396-2-0

HERBARY BOOKS

Published by Herbary Books
Caernarfon, Wales

www.herbarybooks.com

contact@herbarybooks.com

Dedication

This book is dedicated to Bob without whom I would not be the person I am today.

Contents

Introduction

Today on Facebook I read "Let it go... one of the happiest moments in life is when you find the courage to let go of what you cannot change". Well maybe – I suppose. If someone very dear to you is developing dementia you cannot change the illness but you can change your attitude to it and that helps. You might be able to laugh at the silly things they do and you might, despite everything, find moments of happiness. But at other times you are just so full of sadness and tiredness from looking after them that 'acceptance' and 'letting go' are just words that make you want to spit and say "How dare anyone tell me to accept this situation. How dare they say there is nothing to be done, there is no cure".

Even now – and it's over nine years since his death – I have struggled to write the story of my life with Bob; the man who became, despite all his problems and failings, my dearest friend and lover.

My story is not just about dementia but about love. I hope that in telling this very personal story I may help to give a greater understanding of the day to day difficulties of looking after a loved one with dementia. I have strived to be very honest and I hope this honesty will help others who may be going through a similar experience.

Bob with Baby Amber

Bob in 2001, In the garden of my Penzance home

Chapter 1

The Beginning

We met first many years ago when my two children were still quite little. I was happily married to John and living in a small village in the far south west of Cornwall. We were quite involved in our local church. John rang the bells and I helped with the youth group and also helped the vicar with his pastoral work by visiting people in the village who were ill or who had other troubles. I had done a short counselling course and thought of myself as able to offer a friendly listening ear.

I first met Bob because he offered to sing in the chorus of a musical version of the story of 'Noah' that we put on in the church.

I remember a tall, good looking man eating cake and chatting to someone in the church hall after the show. I may have said "hello" to him but that was the limit of our conversation.

Months passed by and it was almost Christmas. John was outside our house and met Bob walking along the road. He started chatting to John and confided in him that he found Christmas a difficult time as he had no family. So John invited him to come and eat with us on Boxing Day.

Boxing Day came and Bob had dinner with us and played with the children and after they had gone to bed, he stayed to chat. He was obviously so happy to have people to talk to. I really can't remember exactly what we all talked about. I remember he told us of his adventures backpacking and sometimes climbing in the mountains in Wales. I know he also talked about more philosophical and spiritual matters. He asked about our beliefs, our philosophy of life and I remember thinking that he talked about all the sorts of things that I found really interesting. I felt as though we talked the same language.

It was getting late by the time he went and I seem to remember John commenting that Bob obviously 'liked to talk'.

Well, I thought to myself, he might 'like to talk' but I had really enjoyed the conversion. I could see he was lonely and I suppose I thought, as I planted a little goodbye kiss on his cheek, that he might be another person to add to my list of people in need of a 'friendly listening ear'. Oh dear!

The next day we received a card thanking us both. I still have it... It was a picture of some poppies and somehow seemed to say so much more than what it actually did say, so much so that I wrote this poem.

***

What on earth possessed me to write this poem? I have no idea. I never showed it to anyone at the time but looking back at it now, it was almost prophetic.

I had told Bob to come over anytime but after a month of not seeing him anywhere I found out where he lived and called round. I was very nervous of doing so but something propelled me up the road to the grotty flats at the back of the pub. It was 2 p.m. when I knocked on his door and a muffled voice said, please would I come back in half an hour. He was obviously still in bed. I wandered around and then went back. A very embarrassed and dishevelled Bob opened the door.

"I've brought you a present."

I gave him a pot of my homemade jam.

"I wondered how you were. I haven't seen you around."

The room was very bare. There was nowhere to sit; one small bed, one cupboard and a small work surface with a baby belling cooker and a small sink. The walls were high and dark and looked damp. I took it all in as I sat down on one end of the bed and Bob sat hunched at the other end. I remember he made me a cup of tea and thanked me profusely for the jam. We both felt

Say it with Flowers

Say what you want
with a wild field full,
or a big bouquet,
but why send poppies?
Are we to meet on the battlefield
after the Holocaust?
Or are you after something everlasting?
I still have two arms, two legs,
and more, I'm not dead
yet if it's passion you want
then send me a rose of deepest red,
or sweet peas for tenderness.
I'll take primroses for friendship,
but when you say it with poppies,
who knows where it may end.

very awkward. He apologised for the state of the flat and for still being in bed when I arrived.

"I've not been sleeping well," he said. "I've been rather down."

I reminded him that he was welcome to come over to our house sometime for a cup of tea and a chat and with that I left.

Gradually, Bob became more confident that I had meant what I said and began to turn up at least once a week. Mostly I sat and listened while Bob talked and talked about his life. Some of the things he told me about were so awful they almost made my hair stand on end. I could write another whole book about them. There is no room here. Gradually he unburdened himself of a lot of the shitty things that had happened to him in his life and he began to lighten up and smile and laugh. But he also liked to philosophise about the meaning of life and so we would have long discussions.

Our backgrounds were so different. His father was killed at Dunkirk and at the end of the war his mother married again. This man was violent to his mother, particularly if he'd had a drink. Seven year old Bob hated to see his mother being hit. He would stand in the way and try to protect her and his stepfather hated him for it. His mother must have decided he'd be safer living somewhere else. She had no relatives, having been brought up by nuns in a home for illegitimate children, so she did what she thought would be best. She sent him to a Catholic children's home in another part of Birmingham, where unfortunately he suffered a lot worse abuse. So he was brought up as a Catholic, mostly by nuns. Once he was an adult he rejected any religion that might try to tell him what to do and was therefore attracted to Quaker faith and practise which has no creed except to say that there is 'that of God in every man'.

I had been brought up on a farm in the Isle of Man by enlightened middle class parents who had an eclectic view of religion: basically a mixture of Quaker, Church of England and Buddhist beliefs. Bob and I had some lively discussions!

Once I remember I said that we should learn to trust more.

He said, "Yes, trust in yourself".

"I meant trust in God."

He said he had great difficulty with the word 'God'.

I said that for me God and my Higher Self meant the same thing, but for Bob 'God' represented the Catholic repressive, judgemental God of his childhood.

"Well for me the word 'God' means the spirit within each of us and also outside of us, but not separate from us, for we are part of this amazing world of nature and for me 'God' is in everything around us, all of creation."

I remember showing Bob my little book of sayings from the 'White Eagle' movement called 'The Quiet Mind'. After initially poo-pooing this little book, he became interested because I would let the book fall open at any page and often it seemed to pour balm into his troubled mind. So I bought him a copy. He particularly liked the page that said, "Keep on keeping on".

Sometimes he would stay an extra hour. I would play the piano and he would sing. He had an amazingly powerful voice. I said he should have been an opera singer but he said that he had never wanted to work at singing in such a disciplined way. He had suffered far too much discipline as a child. Sometimes he'd stay and play games with my children when they returned from school.

I well remember my daughter, Kira, trying to show him some of the dance steps she was learning for ballet. Picture a big, rather clumsy man trying to stand on one leg and pirouette. We all fell about laughing, Bob included, as he collapsed in a heap on the lawn.

I didn't mean to fall in love with Bob. I saw him as a good friend who was in need of a bit of help but then he had such a strong physical presence and somehow, even though I had only ever held his hand, I began to realise just how powerfully I felt about him. Somehow we both talked about our feelings and found that we both felt the same. He was ready to flee.

"You're married. I can't do anything that would harm your marriage to John."

Hand in Hand

Under a threatening sky,
they walked hand in hand.
Looking into the clear water
the green weeds flowed
with the movement of the river.
'What shall we do?' he said.
'Throw ourselves in,' she said
'it may wash some sense into us.'
'It is too deep,' he said 'and cold
but not as deep as we both run.'
'Let's go on,' she said and so
they wandered on and on
while clouds gathered above
and the sharp brambles caught at their legs.
Rain fell as a flock of crows flew by,
and the wind rose under the darkening sky.

So we left it at that, though it was very hard for both of us. I so wanted Bob. It was around this time I wrote this poem.

I also wanted to help Bob in practical ways too. I had an idea. I had some money that was sitting in a savings account. I could buy a little cottage and let it to Bob for a very reasonable rent, so he wasn't in that horrible flat anymore.

I had been writing about my feelings for him in my private diary, not realising that John was in the habit of reading it. When I wrote this idea, John spoke to me.

"What's going on?"

"What do you mean?"

"Well, I've been reading your diary and I see you're writing about buying a house to let to Bob!"

"So you know all about my feelings for Bob?"

"Yes," he said, "but I haven't fancied you for years anyway".

I felt such a mixture of anger, humiliation and hurt. Did John really care so little for me? How dare he read my diary! Why was I trying so hard to behave myself with Bob? I certainly wasn't going to anymore! I sat in stunned silence. Nothing else was said. We went to bed in an uneasy silence and I think I hardly slept.

It wasn't long after this that I persuaded Bob to come away with me for a few days and soon after that I thought I should leave John for Bob but my children wept when I told them. I was heartbroken. I couldn't hurt them and ruin their lives. I knew I had to put my children first. After this Bob moved out of the village so we wouldn't see each other so easily. John and I had counselling to help us patch our marriage up. John said he still loved me and so I did my best to put Bob out of my mind and start over again...

Months passed. I tried to forget him but I felt as if something inside me was dying from lack of nourishment. I missed him so much. I had found in Bob someone I could really talk to. Someone I could trust so much that I felt able to share my deepest feelings, my deepest fears and some pretty awful skeletons. Bob, having suffered so much himself, was very understanding of others and completely un-shockable and not at all judgemental. How I missed our talks.

One day, I received a letter from Bob. He sounded so sad, just really down. So I jumped in the car and went straight round to see him. From then on, we kept in touch and I regularly popped in to see him. I never wrote in my diary about him anymore, in case John read it and I never talked to anyone about our friendship except for a very few close friends. I know that many will judge me for having this clandestine relationship but I loved Bob with a passion that I had never felt in my life before and he loved me with a similar intensity. I know it was wrong to live this 'double life'. I am not trying to excuse myself, but that is what happened. I didn't want to hurt my children or John but maybe I should have had the courage to leave John sooner rather than years later.

So, about once a week, we'd meet for lunch at Bob's flat and sometimes we would go for walks together on the moor or along the coast, lost in deep discussions or having passionate moments under trees or on the cliff tops. From time to time I would see him at the café in Penzance where he often helped his friend Peter with the cooking. He had made friends there, and when he wasn't cooking, he would enjoy a game of chess. He also made friends with a lovely woman called Jan who worked in a book shop. Recently, I asked Jan to write to me with some of her memories of Bob and this is what she wrote:

"I remember chess evenings where we never actually finished a game but wandered into conversation about world beliefs and then of course Bob educated me in classical music! It was the era of the CDs produced by Naxos to make classical music more affordable. Bob was delighted by the quality of them and we would often listen to his latest acquisition. I have several CDs he gave me and seeing them always reminds me of him. He introduced me to the glories of Bach and of course opera!

A vivid memory is of one evening when I was closing up at the bookshop and Bob dropped by. In the fading winter afternoon light, he gave me a rendition of E Lucevan Le Stelle from Tosca. I can still hear it in my memory. It was so powerful and from then on I was hooked by opera!

A treasured gift from Bob is 'The Quiet Mind', the little book of sayings from White Eagle. I have found it so helpful through the sad times. "Keep on keeping on," as Bob used to often say..."

***

Years passed, my children grew into teenagers. I was busy working as a chiropodist and reflexologist. John was busy working as an engineer. We jogged along together. We were good friends. We never fell out but we were a bit like tramlines. His main hobby was amateur dramatics. He was a very good actor. I mainly enjoyed walking, writing, painting pictures and growing vegetables in my garden. We met for meals after work and would ask each other if we'd had a good day and talk about this and that, laugh and joke a bit but we never really communicated at a heartfelt level.

During this time, Bob had a heart attack. It wasn't a serious one but I was very worried about him. My daughter, Kira, who was now nearly seventeen, found me crying quietly in the bathroom.

"Why are you crying, Mum? Mum?"

"A friend of mine has had a heart attack and I'm very worried. What if he'd died...?"

Somehow she guessed. "It's Bob, isn't it?"

"Yes."

"I want to see him," she announced. "I always loved Bob".

We drove to his flat. I went in ahead of her.

"Kira wants to see you, she's outside."

"I would love to see her," said Bob and then Kira came in and gave him an enormous hug. She hadn't seen him for about five years.

It was a great comfort to feel I had the support of my older daughter.

In the summer of 1999 John was rehearsing for a play that was to be performed at the Minack open air theatre. At the end of the week of performances he told me that he'd fallen in love with one of the other actors and intended to leave me. He had fallen in love and had fleeting affairs once or twice before but this time it sounded more serious. "She is the love of my life," he said.

I should have told him then and there that it was okay, that I had been seeing Bob, but I was a coward and said nothing. I just wasn't that upset and so I think he guessed. I finally was able to see Bob openly. My children were almost grown up. They didn't seem surprised that their parents were splitting up.

"You should have done it sooner," they said.

***

I found it very hard to leave John. We had known each other for about thirty years and been married for over twenty six of those years. We were determined to stay friends whatever. We were both guilty of being unfaithful. We split everything equally between us and sold the big old family home and moved to two small cottages in Penzance. By now Kira was living with her partner Ariel and had two babies under two: Amber and Jasper. I spent time with them whenever I could. My younger daughter Alexis was at college and was also looking to live independently and she eventually moved into a flat nearby. It was a very busy time. The cottage needed some renovating and I needed builders and plumbers and electricians. I had to relocate my chiropody and reflexology business to a room above a health food shop. I had had a room in our big family home that I had worked from before. Bob carried on living in his flat but spent a lot of time coming over to stay with me. He had a pension now and so he didn't need to work or look for work. He liked to cook and clean and generally help where ever he could. He was a very good cook but when it came to putting up shelves it was generally accompanied with a few curses, usually after he'd hit his thumb with a hammer or banged his head on the door post. And everything had to be screwed on with so many screws that I think it would have taken an earthquake to move the shelves. It became a joke between us.

"You like screwing!" I would giggle and he would give me a cheeky grin.

He offered to knock a wall down in order to help me move the piano out of the conservatory and into the main house. Fortunately I found a builder to do it! Goodness knows what might have happened if Bob had done it. I began to realise how lucky I had been all those years having such a very capable and practical husband. Bob's heart was in the right place but he definitely wasn't quite so competent!

Bob's friend, Jan, was so pleased that I was now living in Penzance and she often came with us, especially if we were going to a concert or to the theatre as I was the only one who drove a car. Bob had a motorbike but had never taken his car driving test.

Another old friend of mine, Peggy, had moved into sheltered accommodation close to my cottage so I was able to pop in to see her regularly and help her in one way or another when I had time. She had very bad emphysema and had been house bound in the upstairs room of her little cottage in Marazion but she now had a lift and a wheel chair and after a few months she had the doctor's permission to leave her oxygen bottle for a few hours, so Bob and I were able to take her on outings around the town. Peggy adored Bob and liked to call him "Muscles". Bob would sit by her bedside for an hour or so chatting away until she would tell him she was tired and needed to sleep. I would like to sit and listen to them chatting. I knew most of Bob's story but there was often yet more to find out. He had moved so many times in his life and had done so many different jobs and also met many interesting people. Freedom to do whatever, to go wherever, had always been so very important to him after his traumatic childhood of being incarcerated in that terrible children's home.

He had been to university where he studied law but after two years he left when his mother, who had been his only anchor, died. He didn't get on very well with his sister or his stepbrother. They had never been close, partly because he had lived so much of his childhood away from home. After a few years he lost touch with them. He never settled anywhere for long after that, and although he had a few girlfriends they never lasted.

He trained as a chef and worked in country hotels all over Scotland and Wales. When he wasn't working, he would go backpacking and sometimes tried rock climbing. Once he worked as a film projectionist, once in a steel works. For seven years he worked as a grave digger and for several as a navy, digging trenches for cables in the Scottish Highlands.

As he got older he moved back to a comfortable council flat in Birmingham. He set up a gardening round, mowing lawns and cutting hedges but he became more and more 'lost'. He felt as if he was in a 'dark and obscure place'. He had always lived in his own way 'like a leaf drifting in the wind,' but now this leaf seemed to be losing it. He felt he was in a prison cell, but the cell was inside his head. He felt more and more that if he didn't move, he would go mad.

One day, he just upped and left. He packed his rucksack with a few essentials: A tent, his sleeping bag, a change or two of clothes, his waterproofs, and a few essential documents and a bank card. He left money for the month's rent on the table and posted the keys and a letter to the council. He didn't tell his few friends where or what he was doing. He didn't know. He just walked. He said that he kept thinking of the far south west of Cornwall. He'd never been there but thought it sounded interesting but somehow he ended up in Oxford.

He took a job working in a hotel as a kitchen porter but he was so disgusted by the poor standards of hygiene in the kitchen that after two or three weeks he went to see the manager and complained and said that he was leaving. She said that he'd agree to work for at least a month and that he was breaking his contract, so he could leave without pay. He was furious. He threatened to 'set about the filthy kitchen' with the meat cleaver if she didn't pay him. So she did!

After that, he did walk to the far end of Cornwall. He tried to find work but it was autumn and the tourists had gone home so there was none. He got as far as Mousehole and set up his camp in the disused Coastguard lookout hut. He made friends with another homeless man and for a short while they shared the lookout hut until they were both moved on by the Coastguard. And that is how he came to live in the grotty flat behind the pub in my village.

The very first time we took Peggy out in her wheelchair it was September 11th 2001. It was to be Peggy's first day out for two years and we were going to take her shopping in her wheelchair. It was a beautiful sunny autumn day. The gas man came to change my faulty gas cooker just before we left and muttered something about a plane crash in New York but we were in a hurry to get away and hardly took in what he was saying... but as we walked into Peggy's flat she had the T.V. on and we saw the New York tower burning and watched as the second of the twin towers was hit by another aeroplane. It was so horrific we sat stupefied. It just didn't seem real. After a few minutes however, we said, "Come on Pegs, it's a lovely day," and helped her into her wheelchair. So we left the Towers to burn and the people for whom we could do nothing. We shut the door and went out into the sunshine and enjoyed our day.

Peggy was like a little child, out for her first shopping spree and full of excitement and joy and calling out to Bob as he pushed her large form in the wheelchair up the Penzance streets, "Come on, Muscles!"

We sped from shop to shop, her happiness spreading itself around to all the other shoppers. She bought little things like some picture frames and soap and then we went to clothes shops where she bought a pair of trousers and some new nighties.

We stopped at last at a café with a great view of St Michael's Mount and ordered naughty cream teas which Peggy was determined to have despite her doctor's orders... and they were very yummy and good.

The reality of the Twin Towers sank in later. The T.V. reports saw to that.

Chapter 2

Moving House and Settling in

Gradually the house is picked apart,
a knitted sweater gone to holes
where pictures hung and books took up
the space on shelves
and all the paraphernalia of place
is parcelled up and taped.

In July 2002, after selling my cottage in Penzance, Bob and I moved to North Wales. We had spent several short holidays there and had been discussing the possibility for a while. My older daughter, Kira, and her partner Ariel had moved to Lancashire with their two very small children and I knew she was struggling emotionally and would need a bit of support at times. So I would be nearer her. Also property was so cheap. I would be able to pay off my debts and still buy somewhere big enough so that Bob could have his own pad.

We would never be able to totally live together. Bob had been a bachelor all his life. We loved each other but we needed to be independent. We were both free spirits. I knew I would miss Cornwall terribly as I had lived there for over 30 years, but moving to Wales was the best thing for Bob. He had been there many times when he was younger, sometimes by bus or on his motorbike but often cycling all the way from Birmingham or from wherever he was living at the time.

He often backpacked over the mountains for days on end, camping or staying in youth hostels. He loved North Wales and I had fallen in love with it on the few holidays we'd had there, walking over mountains and through valleys or swimming in the lakes. Most important of all, though, was that we were making a new start in life together.

I would still have to commute to Cornwall for a while until I found a buyer for my chiropody business but I wasn't too worried about that. A local chiropodist was going to help me out for a few months and I could stay with my younger daughter Alexis in her big basement flat.

Soon after we arrived, we wrote to friends in Cornwall. Bob, rolling out his love of words, like he always did, wrote to his friend Jan.

Dear Jan,

....it has not been all work. We have found time to get out onto the mountains (by simply downing tools and leaving the work) – on two beautiful days, on which the sun shone as if for our particular delight and we have already climbed two major mountains, one on our own doorstep – Craig Cwm Silyn, and, because Ali wanted keenly to make her acquaintance, Snowdon herself.

Craig Cwm Silyn found us woefully unfit, and we made heavy weather of this first ascent, despite the mountain being only 2408 feet. For all that she is the centrepiece of a most magnificent and sustained ridge walk girding the Nantlle valley in which we live. Getting up to the peak was hard as the contours are closely packed and the climb unrelenting – worth getting up there however, as Snowdon and all the other major peaks are arrayed before one! We felt better and fitter for the experience and will definitely explore the other seven peaks, and also others which make up this beautiful mountain playground. The books describe the Nantlle Ridge as "quiet" and "lonely" but very rewarding, which suits us down to the ground!

Ali has always wanted to climb Snowdon, but never done so. Well today we did, and I took Ali on the Miner's Track which I did last – many years ago – perhaps twenty five – an age ago! It showed in my forgetting a lot of it, partly because the tracks on the mountain have been improved out of all recognition under the sheer impact of the lust for access to these mountains in general, but in particular to Snowdon itself. The work done is sustained and very sophisticated and it shows when the sun comes out and people want to play! Years ago I viewed any interference askance, feeling I was being controlled! I'm afraid I was ignorant and uninformed! If the mountains are to be preserved as a heritage for all, then they must be looked after and maintained! It's amazing what a difference a quarter of a century can make! I am myself one of the 'hordes,' the tourists who come to places like this to renew themselves and escape, if only briefly, much in our modern life that tends to deny such needs in favour of a supposedly greater uniformity that offers to all of us EVERYTHING that we could possibly need!

Ali and I saw an invalid, (note the word in – valid, no use!) being pushed along by her friends and loving every minute of it, transcending her state in an afternoon of pleasure and joy.

We also met an elderly couple from Anglesey with whom we talked along the track for a while before going ahead. They did not think they would attain the summit. They called us mountain goats and urged us on. The lady's husband confided to me that his wife 'couldn't do much these days'. Later when we had reached the summit and stood upon 'the roof of Wales' we met them again, elated, having done what they had never thought to do – to gain the world in a single afternoon! The lady said that when she looked up at the way she had to go she thought she would 'never climb that!' But she did.

"I said to Vince, 'just let me do a bit more' and that bit added to another bit and then to my amazement I'd done it!"

On the way down we kept company with them for a little while, but then they urged us on – we 'mountain goats!' We kept looking back, worrying a little but they appeared, with Ali's binoculars trained upon them, and we waved to them over the distance and they waved back and we walked on.

I thought about this 'Miner's Track' and of the path, seemingly different, that all of us must tread – aware or unaware; and I thought of the simple phrase of White Eagle's "keep on keeping on!"

On this note I must close or I shall never finish – and look forward to seeing you when we come down again soon.

With love from us both,
Bob xxx

My letter was shorter.

Dear Peggy,

We love it here. We can see Snowdon from the garden! The garden is half an acre of land which is really more like a field with one very friendly Aylesbury duck called 'Quack'. She came with the house and has a voracious appetite for house scraps. She has so far laid four rather odd shaped eggs. We have both fallen in love with her and are going to build her a proper pond. The baby bath left behind by the previous owners seems a bit inadequate.

Bob has been worrying about getting housing benefit now that we share a house but this house is perfect for us both as he has a self-contained flat, (his cave) to retreat to and the man from the council came to inspect it and was well content. So Bob is now very happy to feel he can contribute towards running costs with his rent.

We are coming back to Penzance next week to pick up the rest of our stuff in the trailer and Bob wants to paint his old flat and leave it spick and span before he hands it back to the agent. He also has this mad idea to bring the Honda 90 in the trailer and then ride on it all the way back to North Wales! Crazy man!! I mean for goodness sake... he's sixty five and he had a heart attack a few years ago but you know how stubborn he is...

Anyway, we will pop in to see you next week for a final farewell... though I will be coming down regularly for a while to do my chiropody until I find someone to take over from me.

Lots of love
Ali and Bob Xx

***

Two weeks later we drove back to Cornwall towing the large trailer with Bob's Honda 90 on board. It was a nightmare of a journey. The bike kept shifting and had to be repositioned several times but before we had even gone a mile, we had to turn around because he'd forgotten his helmet and his waterproofs. I was knackered before we'd even started. Then it lashed with rain and then Bob got a blinding headache. He never got headaches and after we arrived back in Cornwall he still didn't seem quite himself.

He kept stumbling over his words a little and he had never done that before. He'd always been so erudite... I was worried that he might have had a slight stroke and I insisted he went to see his old doctor, but she said he'd got nothing to worry about and that it was just the stress of moving. I remember thinking that he should have asked for tests to make sure, but Bob hated medical interference of any sort and I suppose I also thought that probably the doctor was right. Bob was so strong and well. It was just stress and there was no need to fret.

We packed the trailer with the remainder of our stuff and covered it with a large tarpaulin tied down extremely thoroughly and parked it on a friend's driveway. Bob then painted his flat and gave his keys in to the agent. He always liked to leave everything better than the way he'd found it. That was Bob's way. Then he gave me a kiss goodbye and set off for North Wales on his little old Honda 90. I remember saying anxiously as he left, "You will stop somewhere on the way... it is 400 miles and you've got money for a B&B". He didn't answer me. I knew he saw it as a challenge and wanted to try and do it without stopping, but it seemed crazy to me. The next day he phoned to say that he'd made it as far as Betws y Coed and then the Honda had died. He had to leave it at a local garage and had got a lift to Caernarfon. Then he walked the eight miles home from there. He said he was tired! I felt tired just thinking about it!

Bob was nine years older than me but he always seemed so young for his age. He was such a tough, big and strong man. Apart from his slight heart attack I don't think he'd ever had a day's illness. I admired his strength. He could pick up rocks as big as himself when I first knew him. I felt so protected when I was with him. He would insist on doing all the heavy lifting. He would hold doors open for me and hold my hand to cross the road. "Give us your paw," he'd always say as he took my hand. I was his little woman and although I was quite tough myself it was wonderful to feel so protected.

I was busy with my chiropody work for the next ten days and stayed with my daughter, Alexis in her large, rather damp basement flat. Then I waved goodbye to Cornwall and towed the trailer back to North Wales.

For the next few months I travelled to and from Cornwall many times: two week's work in Cornwall and then two weeks back home with Bob. He worked so hard while I was away. We had decided to have oil fired central heating installed but it was very expensive. Bob tried to persuade me to stick with the coal fired central heating, but it was old and kept breaking down and I pointed out that we weren't getting any younger and might not be able to hump coal in ten years' time. So to save money, Bob dug the trench for the oil pipe, from the oil tank to the house. It turned into an enormous job as it seemed as if every rock in North Wales conspired to be in the way of the trench, but eventually it was done. After that he set about painting the house, inside and out.

We didn't always get on. We did things differently. I liked to get things done – like yesterday – and often I would act and then think afterwards. Bob liked to ponder, to talk and discuss everything. When he did then act, things had to be done perfectly, with almost 160% perfection, let alone 100% and they had to be done in his way or not at all.

"Stubborn old thing!" I called him. Also, with me being away in Cornwall working, he was left looking after the whole house and as my side was bigger and more comfortable, I would come back to a Bob who seemed not to use his end of the house much at all – except when Kira and her family came to stay when he would retreat 'bear-like' into his end (his cave) to escape the noisy chaos of the family. I felt I had no place of my own. Where did our divisions lie? He didn't like me to use his place but had taken over mine!

We also had a heated discussion about money. Although I was away a lot, I had agreed to pay all the bills: the food, the heating, the rates, the house insurance etc. in return for all his hard work. Then I was also spending out on a new boiler, paint, plaster etc. He had never owned a house. He said that he felt I was being unfair to still charge him rent. I pointed out that I was ending up with less and less money while he was saving his money. I also said that he was enjoying the whole house and me!

Whenever I was up in Wales, I missed my family and my friends in Cornwall even though I was going down there to work. I still felt the wrench. New friends are not made overnight and friends have always been important to me. Travelling to and fro was unsettling and tiring and I went down with a really horrible cold.

Feeling thoroughly grumpy, I wrote a silly poem to cheer myself up.

***

Cheer up Poem

The garage roof is leaking,
the computer has gone dead.
The phone is always ringing
and I have an aching head.

The wind is howling at the door
and beating on the pane,
and rather like old Cornwall,
it's rain, rain, rain!

But the house roof isn't leaking
and the windows all have glass,
and I have a strong and handsome man
who likes to stroke my ass.

So I'm really not complaining,
though I miss my old friends dear,
and I miss the coast of Cornwall –
but I'm better off up here.

The winter nights were closing in. It was November and I had some good news. A young man called Alex was taking over my chiropody practice and paying me a good price. So there would be no more commuting to Cornwall every two weeks. I'd miss the money but I was starting to get some work nearby. I bought a new chiropody bag and we celebrated the sale of my business by going out for an 'Indian' as Bob loved hot curry and I wanted to treat him.

A few days later we went to see a very interesting play. It was called 'Ta-ra Teresa' and was half in Welsh and half in English. We had headphones to help with the Welsh bits. It was a bit like a light-hearted Romeo and Juliet, only one family was Welsh and the other was English.

We were both keen to learn Welsh and planned to start classes after Christmas. I'd have my chiropody business in Cornwall completely sewn up by then — great!

It was so nice to be settling into my home and not always travelling. I bought ingredients for making chutney with some apples one of our lovely new friends had given us. I also bought stuff for making Christmas puddings and cake. Our first Christmas together in our new home would be coming soon and I wanted to make it special.

At the beginning of December I went up to Lancashire to be with my family for a few days. Bob didn't want to come. He was intent on finishing the painting and Andy, our neighbour, was coming over to help him fit a new back door. I loved playing with my grandchildren, Amber and Jasper, and it gave Kira and Ariel a break. I enjoyed taking the children out on trips to the woods and to the farm park where they could feed the animals. Jasper was a bit nervous of some of the bigger creatures but they both loved the guinea pigs and the pigmy goats.

While I was away I wrote in my diary:

"Bob has just rung me and he talked and talked and talked. He went on at length about what he was cooking and how, then about Andy (our neighbour) and how he had cut the wood wrong for the door and got very

upset about it. Probably Bob was talking so much that Andy couldn't think straight! Anyway Bob says things and then says the same things again and then again. He's always tended to repeat himself but he seems to be doing it a lot more nowadays so I'm afraid I ended up only half listening and reading an article in a magazine at the same time. I'm finding I have to accept a lot about Bob that is difficult. I do love him but he is getting so forgetful – more and more like an absent-minded professor. It's annoying at times and also a bit worrying. I've just written a silly poem – having a laugh helps me to see things in perspective. I'm sure I am worrying unnecessarily.

Anyway, Amber and Jasper are playing with "boons" – the balloons I bought them yesterday, so I shall go back to playing too. Kira and Ariel are out selling 'Clean easy' door to door.

***

Christmas 2002 was to be a first for me in many ways: our first Christmas in Wales, my first Christmas just with Bob and my first Christmas without any members of my family.

It was a busy time. I had been determined to get the house looking more like my own. Since we'd moved in July, Bob had been digging trenches from the oil tank to the house so we could have oil fired central heating installed. He'd painted the whole of the outside of the house white and yellow and it looked lovely. It had been green. We'd also painted most of the interior which had also been green, a deep green that took at least three coats to cover it over. We joked that we were 'de-greening' the house, but it was no joke! Even the curtains and carpets left by the previous owners were green – they were mostly quite nice so we kept them.

Bob and I wrote Christmas cards and letters to all our friends in Cornwall and elsewhere and I also dropped cards off to our new neighbours and friends inviting them to a little Christmas party on the 27th December at our freshly 'de-greened' house! I was sure they would be curious to see what we had been doing to the old place and I did want to use it as a way of saying thank you to them all for the way they had welcomed us into their little community.

Accept Your Man

If you plan to leave at 10 o'clock
accept it will be 12 o'clock
before you get away to town.
And it you hurry him or frown,
you will find it takes still longer,
the excuses getting stronger
that he forgot his glasses,
his cheque book or his passes
for the library and the bus.

So don't sigh or make a fuss
when plans go awry.
Accept that he's forgetful,
but in other ways so helpful,
like cooking up the yummiest apple pie!

I wrote a long letter to Peggy in Cornwall.

Dear Peggy,

How are you? I hope you're being good and obeying doctor's orders and staying out of the cold and damp!

Bob and I often talk of you and miss you and I know last time I phoned I woke you up so I thought I'd write for a change and enclose your Christmas card.

We are very happy in Wales and have just made some new friends. We went to a Quaker meeting twice and there we met Gillian and Holger and their son Dafydd. Holger is from East Germany and speaks English with a strong accent – difficult to understand him but he's such a gentle sweet guy. His partner Gillian is blond and vivacious and comes from Chorley and knows friends of mine from there – what a small world it is! They live quite near us too, so that's nice.

The Bangor Quakers are all very friendly. I think we shall go there quite often.

We also went to the 'Nine Lessons and Carols' service at the cathedral. Bangor Cathedral is squat, more like a big church, but the choir sang beautifully and we sang lots of carols very heartily and went home with carols in our hearts and piles of food in the boot. Just enough time to grab a bite to eat and go to Talysarn St. Ioan church for their little concert at 6:30. The band played and we sang more carols, mostly in Welsh and a small group of children re-enacted the Christmas story, mostly reading in Welsh in front of a very static Mary and Joseph. Three boys with tea towels on their heads plonked a fluffy toy lamb by the manger and then three wise men with paper crowns dropped off their gifts.

A little girl played the flute, struggling to keep up with the pianist. It was all very simple but lovely, like the little church itself.

Talysarn used to have four large chapels and this little church, all full to the brim in the heyday of the busy working quarries. The population was probably four times larger than it is now. Now the quarries are returning to nature. The deep holes have become enormously deep lakes where divers explore the deeps and sometimes come to grief. The quarry buildings are ruins overrun with trees and wildlife – and everywhere there is a sort of eerie beauty.

Between painting the house and cooking Christmas puddings, mince pies and cake, Bob and I have been very busy. We've dropped off invitations to all our neighbours and new friends to come to a little party here on the 27th. I hope it goes okay.

It's wild and windy outside and it's getting late. I must feed Quack, our pet duck, and put her to bed. Then there is brandy butter to make.

Bob is sitting beside me reading a very interesting book, so he says: "Family, life, birth, death and the whole damn thing" – I suspect he's swatting up on how to cope with me and my family, poor man!

I hope you have a peaceful Christmas, dear Pegs. Take care my dear, and I shall come down to see you when the weather is better in the spring. 'Muscles' sends you a big, big hug!

Lots of love from us both,
Ali

***

Christmas day was peaceful. We watched a bit of television and ate too much so we had a walk up to the lakes below Cwm Silyn. The Christmas party on the 27th went well too. Our nearest neighbours, Andy and Deb, also had a party to celebrate New Year. They had been particularly kind and helpful to us. Andy was so practical and would come and help us with all sorts of little problems that Bob and I were not very good at solving and Deb was such a lovely friendly person.

Kira and family came to stay for a few days after New Year. It was nice weather so the first day we all went to the beach. The children wanted their 'Bobby' to help build lots of sandcastles, so two massive forts were constructed, one for each of them. Meanwhile I collected pebbles and shells for decoration. Kira and Ariel went off for a walk. Later, when we came home, Bob and Ariel cooked while Kira and I did finger painting with the children. The next day we all went out to Cwm Pennant and had a walk by the river. It was a lovely sunny day – wonderful after so much dark and dull weather. Later that day, Kira threw a wobbly with the children. Jasper, in particular, had been so very difficult but she seemed to get so overwhelmed that I was worried about her mental state. I just had to hope and pray that things would improve. I so wanted both to help but not be an interfering grandmother.

After the family had gone home Bob was very tense and was not sleeping well. He was probably worrying about Kira and the grandchildren or worrying about me worrying about them, one or other or both. We had talked about meditation in the past as I meditated every day and had found it a wonderful tool, helping me to see things in perspective and helping me to relax and let go of my worries. Bob said he'd been thinking about this for a while and had now decided he would like to learn how to do it. So I gave him a few simple lessons and it did seem to be helping him to relax.

The weather helped too. It was so beautiful, frosty and bright and we were able to get out and walk on the mountains. We needed a compass and map at times though, especially when the mist descended. We both needed to work at our skills in orienteering. Bob reckoned he knew how to do it but when we were out and the mist came down he was a bit fazed by it and blamed his long-sightedness on not being able to read the compass and the map properly. I had told him he should always have his glasses with him, but he just hated the fact that he needed them at all. He seemed to believe that if he denied there was any problem with anything health related, that he would overcome it and it would just magically go away. This may have worked when he was young and extremely fit but I pointed out that it was not so likely to work for someone in their sixties!

I wrote this poem after one our wonderful mountain walks.

Carnedd Dafydd

I feel wild Earth's first movements here
in phases of the moon, and in the mist
that circulates the seasons year on year
where snow and rain fall down the jagged fist.

I hear the calling raven in this place of bog,
a storm staggered rock strewn land
where we wander like tiny ants in a fog
on the back of a giant's hand.

A wet day in the mountains.

Sometimes Bob needed a lie-in so I would walk up the mountains alone. I loved walking with Bob but on my own I could commune with nature at a much deeper level, feeling at one with everything around me: the feel of the rocks and heather beneath my feet, the smell of the rain coming, the smell of a fox, the sounds of the wind in the dead stalks of grass, the cry of the raven and the sound of my own rucksack creaking slightly. I felt a deep sense of gratitude that Bob and I were living in this beautiful land of Wales.

In the second week of January we joined a Welsh learner's class in Bangor. It was held in an old chapel and we were given books and tapes to help us with the course. We had a lovely Welsh teacher call Nia. We both enjoyed her lessons at first. They mainly involved learning through speaking and a bit of play acting too. After a few weeks Bob did seem to be struggling with the course.

He would come home afterwards and confess to me that he just didn't find it easy.

A few weeks into the course a funny thing happened. It was the end of the lesson and I went to the loo. Nia, our teacher, not realising where I was, went and locked me in. Bob and everyone else had gone. It was an old chapel with high windows. Oh help! I went into the kitchen and propped a chair against the window and climbed up. I saw some students from the university walking down the path about 50 yards away. I banged on the window and then managed to open it and yell. It was lucky they heard me. They went to look for Bob who was sitting in the car listening to his music and wondering where I was! Together they helped me out and lifted me down. We then had to ring the office because we couldn't shut the window. Poor Nia, we teased her about it for weeks!

***

At the end of January another thing happened which was a lovely surprise. My wonderful Bobby bought me a piano! My old one had taken up residence in Alexis' basement flat in Cornwall before we moved. She loved playing the piano too, but I did miss it. I was so happy with the piano and immediately got out my music and played some of my old favourite folk songs and classical pieces too. The weather was foul again so we spent many happy hours reading or listening to music on the CD player. Then I would play my new piano and Bob would sing his heart out. He was a much better singer than I was a pianist.

I loved Bob's singing. He had a wonderful voice and should have been an opera singer but, like so much in his life, he had never let his abilities shine out; having had such a traumatic childhood, it probably knocked his confidence. He loved to sing arias from various operas and his greatest favourites were ones from La Boheme and Tosca, but he also liked folk music, which was more my thing. I had a book of traditional folk songs that I would often play on the piano but I also particularly liked Enya's songs. I had her CDs as well as books of her piano pieces. So I would play the piano and we would sing along together.

One day, while the rain continued to beat on the windows I decided to plan my garden. It was too wet and cold to be doing any digging and anyway I had a headache and a sore throat. Bob kept making me hot cider vinegar and honey drinks to keep the head cold at bay. Meanwhile, I drew a garden plan showing where different flower and fruit and vegetable beds could go. I was reading a book on permaculture while Bob read Viktor Frankl's book, 'Man's Search for Meaning'. Viktor Frankl was an Austrian psychiatrist and also a Holocaust survivor. Bob had always enjoyed reading books that looked deeply into psychological ideas and also religious and non-religious books on the meaning of life. We often read books like this together, discussing them as we went. Recently though, he'd been collecting a supply of lighter novels. Whilst browsing in the charity shops in Caernarfon he'd found some books by Catherine Cookson. They were inspired by her childhood in County Durham during the First World War. He said the stories reminded him of the grinding poverty of his own childhood home.

We sat snuggled by the open fire in his end of the house. In his book lined room there was an old Welsh range in an inglenook with an enormous slate lintel above it. It gave out a good heat if you fed the flames regularly. Bob went out to fetch some more coal from the shed and told me to stay by the fire and keep warm. I could hear the wind howling. Every now and then it would roar down the Nantlle valley from Snowdon, building and building and then it would hit our little hamlet with a Whoomff!! Then our old range would let out a puff of smoke into the room for a moment before righting itself and continuing to send smoke up the chimney. It made me cough a bit and so Bob went off into the kitchen and made us both a hot cup of tea. Then he came back and put the Viktor Frankl book aside and got down his latest Catherine Cookson. He tucked a blanket round me and settled down to sup his tea. He loved to look after me when I wasn't well. I felt so cossetted.

I did find living with Bob difficult sometimes because we were so different, I suppose. He started everything with great enthusiasm but would never settle on one thing for long and would jump ahead in his mind to grandiose dreams of running his own business, owning a bookshop or running a cafe or even going back to university. All his life he had worked hard but at many different jobs. He would stay for a while but then move on to another job, another place, another relationship. Maybe, I hoped, he would find some peace and rest with me in our little hamlet in Wales. He had his own 'cave,' he had his books and his music. We would often walk in the hills and sometimes go out to concerts or to see a film or to have tea with friends, but mostly we were very comfortable and content pottering. I hoped we would both live to a ripe old age enjoying this gentle life together.

One February morning I wrote in my diary:

"I can hear a buzzard calling. Is it my imagination? Maybe it is as it's only just getting light. I have crawled carefully out of bed so as not to wake my Bobby. I'm finding sleeping with him hard this last week or so as he gets up to pee about 3 or 4 a.m. and that wakes me up. My IBS seems to be bad at the moment so then I have to trail to the loo on and off for the rest of the night

with rumbling guts which keeps him awake.

Anyway I'm downstairs now having a hot cup of tea. I have been worrying, lying awake beside him unable to sleep. He is older than me but he has always seemed so young and fit, despite the heart problem. But sometimes he seems so forgetful now and I fear him getting old and going gaga. I hope and pray that he is just mellowing into a happy old age and that he stays in good health. I really mustn't think black thoughts just because it's that 'dark hour before dawn' and I'm not sleeping! It's just negativity brought on by tiredness so pull yourself together girl and suggest that he sleeps in his cave for a few nights at least."

Reading this diary entry now, I can see things from a very different perspective. My worries were not just black thoughts. I feel now that they were possibly premonitions of what was to come. I have always tried to see the positive side of life and fought my battles with a joke or as much good humour as I could muster so although I had these thoughts I wouldn't have allowed myself to dwell on them for too long.

A day or so later I wrote another humorous poem when I'd persuaded Bob that he needed to go to his own bed for a few days so we could both catch up on sleep.

...Such are the imperfections of being in love when you're getting old!

***

Later on in February Bob started to make heavy weather of the Welsh course. I'd hoped and hoped that he wouldn't give it up. It worried me that he was finding it so hard. It seemed easy to me. Worries gnawed away at the back of my mind but I just tried to ignore them. I was busy planning on going to Cornwall for few days to see Alexis and my ex – John. Also I wanted to see old friends, in particular our dear friend Peggy who was very ill. I was worried about her as I knew she could die anytime soon.

Bob was happy to stay at home and look after Quack. He said he'd start digging a plot for the vegetables if the weather was dry.

February Poem

Bob has gone to his own little bed next door.
I can put the light on, even stamp on the floor,
I can sleep through the night like a babe reborn
and jump out of bed at 6 in the morn.
No longer awoken by his stagger to pee,
the hump in the bed that pulls covers off me,
but I've nowhere to put my toes when they're cold,
and there's no loving hands my body to hold.

I'd marked out a rough plan for him. We'd already bought three apple trees and some soft fruit bushes which he helped me plant. Our land was so full of rock and the soil so poor, it would be a miracle if we grew anything much so I'd bought a few bags of compost to help the miracle happen!

It was lovely to see everyone in Cornwall and Peggy got a bit better during my stay. When I first arrived she was in hospital, all tubed up and had been taking a lot of heavy medication. The large quantities of steroids were affecting her eye sight and she was finding it difficult to read, so I sat and read to her. She wanted to know about the book that I was reading: 'The Power of Now' by Eckhart Tolle. She really enjoyed what I read so I bought her an audio set of CDs of the book. She said that she found them very comforting and inspiring to listen to. I was so glad I took the time to go and see her.

While I was away in Cornwall Bob hurt his knee. He ran down the road for the bus and had obviously sprained something as it was really swollen and sore. I was knackered after the long drive home from Cornwall but the next day I drove him to the hospital to have it X-rayed. They said he had sprained the tendons and should rest it. Later we went to the Welsh lesson and afterwards got stuck in a traffic jam on the way home. Some poor soul had had an accident. We stopped for fish and chips in Penygroes. They were very meagre portions. I made a mental note not to go there again. Then a new patient came for treatment. He had an ingrown nail and was a bit deaf. By the end of the day I was even more knackered!

A few days later, Bob got very uptight at the Welsh class. Everything was speeding up, he said, so he did not want go anymore. He said he would go at his own pace using the books and the tapes. I felt sad but more worn out by him going on and on about it. The pain in his knee wasn't helping, especially as he had to rest it and couldn't go out walking or help me in the garden. He holed himself up in the house and was extremely grumpy. It was beautiful weather too.

One day I was digging in the garden and looked up at the sky to see a buzzard flying right above me. Then I saw two and then three and then five buzzards flying right over my head. It was a wonderful sight but were they seeing me as potential meat?

Another morning I woke up to a beautiful day, fed Quack, left a note for Bob who was still asleep and was off. It was so warm for March with not a breath of wind. I walked to the top of Craig Cwm Silyn, our local mountain. It was only 9:45 a.m. when I sat at the top munching dates and biscuits. The only sound was the distant rumble of jets − practising for war in the Middle East I suspected. A war I hoped and prayed wouldn't happen, but here, with all the beauty of Wales around me, it seemed very far away. Looking one way I could see down the coast to Cardigan Bay and looking the other way, I could see Caernarfon with its castle and beyond that the Isle of Anglesey. Behind me were all the bigger mountains of Snowdonia and in front the long thin peninsula of the Llyn.

I sat with my back against a rock and meditated for a while. The breeze suddenly picked up and I wrapped my jacket tighter around me and put my woolly hat on my head. My thoughts wandered and returned to worrying about Bob finding the Welsh lessons so hard. Maybe it was his age, or maybe he just didn't want to be bothered to learn a new language or maybe... oh I just didn't know... but he was getting more forgetful... and then there was his knee problem. The night before, we'd had a lovely time and gone out with some friends to 'Goma in Concert'. He had been able to dance a bit so at least his knee was hopefully on the mend. I told myself to stop worrying and wandered back down the mountain.

Bob was such a stubborn man and kept doing far too much so his knee got worse again. I felt so fed up *for* him but I was fed up with him too. We had to sleep separately because he was restless with the pain and anyway he had always been a bit of a night owl. He liked to go to bed late and get up late. So often we just seemed to be doing different things. It was beautiful weather but he would sit inside reading or listening to music or doing his 'Form study'. Bob was not really a horse betting man but he liked playing with the theory of winning. Form Study is about picking a winning horse by reading the form. Form is the record of a horse's performance in previous races and is seen by many as a good way of predicting a horse's future performance. Comparing horses' form should enable you to pick the likely best performers in a race.

The birds were singing and lambs were running and jumping in the fields and he was inside doing his bloody Form Study! I wrote this poem for him.

***

I gave Bob the poem and then I cried on Bob's shoulder and he gave me a big, big hug. I had been worrying so much but when he held me like that I felt so comforted. Bob had such healing in his hands. There was me, worrying about him, and yet when he held me in such a loving and understanding way, my worries and frustrations about him not being able to keep up at the Welsh class and not being able to come out walking with me and about me missing Cornwall and my old friends so, so much, especially Peggy – all these feelings and emotions were calmed by his unconditional love.

Outside Inside

Let me bring to your room the soft golden light of evening,
the blackbird's song, the sound of lambs and mother sheep
calling to each other in the fields.

Let me bring you the sound of the stream where water bursts
over banks and budding trees, their limbs stretched to branches
and twigs become nests full of chirps and rustles.

Let me bring to you the yellow primrose, green leaf,
ladybird on my finger
and the look of dark eyes inscrutable,
the milky smell of black cattle slowly chewing grass.

The serious business of sandcastles!

Bob feeding Quack a biscuit

Chapter 3

Moving On

In April 2003 Peggy died, and we went back to Cornwall for her funeral where Bob sang the beautiful African American spiritual 'Going Home,' his parting gift to her. He sang so movingly and well, despite being close to tears. I was so proud of him.

We took the opportunity to see old friends and family while we were there and that was good. Several of our old Cornish friends said to me that Bob seemed quieter.

I wrote in my diary:

"I think he has become quieter... He says that sometimes he can't seem to find words and has to think more before he speaks. He says he thinks he has aphasia."

The next few months were busy ones for me. A local chiropodist retired and I took over her clients. Bob's knee was still giving him trouble so I tried to do more of the heavy work around the place. He had various treatments from an osteopath and finally got some treatment on the NHS with a physiotherapist and it did gradually improve.

It was a good summer, hot and sunny for Wales and we worked hard on our garden. We also acquired a cat called Chess from one of my patients who was moving to Spain. Chess was a great character, a big black bruiser of a cat. He would box the local dogs on the backside if they came too close and sit on the garage roof surveying his domain ready to jump down and see off any cat who dared to enter our garden. Bob loved Chess and Chess loved him.

One of the highlights of the summer was our trip to see Bryn

Terfel at the Faenol festival with Gillian and Holger. We drove in convoy and parked near to their old campervan which was a godsend at the end of the concert when we climbed in and had a hot cup of tea and some of Gillian's delicious cake. There was total chaos all around us outside with so many cars trying to get to the exit all at the same time. But we were sat, curled up, cosy and content to wait for the queue of traffic to move. The highlight of the evening for Bob was when the three main singers, Hayley Westenra, Bryn Terfel and Jose Carreras sang Schubert's 'Ave Maria'. Bob was in seventh heaven and sang it over and over again for days afterwards. He had sung 'Ave Maria' many times as a boy in the church of the Catholic home where he was incarcerated. He often said of that terrible place that the one saving grace was the music. He had been the best chorister they had ever had and apparently the nuns said he had the voice of a nightingale.

Autumn was beautiful, sunny and dry. We went cycling a lot as it was better for Bob's knee. We picked loads of blackberries and sloes. Bob loved working in the kitchen and made beautiful jams and chutneys and some sloe gin.

There were ups and downs with my family. Kira and Ariel had been planning to sell their house and move to Spain but then Kira discovered she was pregnant so that idea was put on hold.

Meanwhile, my younger daughter, Alexis had an operation and she came back to our home to convalesce over Christmas. Christmas went in a mad flurry as all the family came to stay, even John, my ex, came up from Cornwall. Bob found it difficult to cope with so many people but it all went okay as long as he could retreat to his 'cave' from time to time.

***

By 2004 I was pretty busy with work. My reputation as the local foot lady had spread and many of my clients were very elderly people who needed me to visit them in their own homes. This took time with a lot of driving up and down tiny lanes and in one particular case, across two fields of sheep on a rickety track. I always took my wellies as I was sometimes wading through mud, opening and closing the gates to keep the sheep in the right fields. At the end of the track there lived a lovely old lady called Jean who was always pleased to see me and always made me a cup of tea to see me on my way. Once or twice over the years my car got stuck in the mud and I had to borrow some old sacking from Jean's shed to help me get back on the road. Residential homes were the easiest option as I could work in the same place for several hours at a stretch: I had regular work at three of these.

After a hard day's work I would often come home to one of Bob's lovely home cooked meals. Bob enjoyed cooking but so did I. He loved buying recipe books from the charity shops and we both liked to try out different recipes on each other.

I would follow the recipe fairly exactly, but Bob never stuck slavishly to a recipe and used ideas from a book as inspiration, a spring board to invent his own recipe. I suggested that he should write his own recipe book. He liked the idea but somehow he never did.

When I was busy with work he liked to spend his days looking for bargains in charity shops, listening to his music or reading. When the weather was nice he would go out walking, wandering the local lanes and paths, singing as he went and calling in to see people in our friendly hamlet. Everyone came to love him and to see him as a colourful character.

He had also bought himself a new motorbike. The Honda 90 never totally recovered from the long trip to North Wales from Cornwall and went for scrap. The new one was a red Yamaha and he loved zooming off on it along the roads that wound around Snowdonia.

Bob's speech was becoming slightly more halting. If he couldn't find the right word he would substitute another, often with amusing results and we would have a giggle over his mistakes and carry on. 'Bob's booboos,' we called them, but sometimes he would be cross with himself. I remember one misty day we were walking on a path near the coast and the sea mist was so thick we could only see a few yards ahead of us. Then suddenly it cleared. Bob called out. "Look over there, Ali, there's the bitch!"

"The bitch?"

"Oh Jesus! I mean the beach of course"

He looked unhappy and said nothing for a while. I kept glancing up at his face and could see he was troubled. We walked on in silence until we reached a stile. The mist had cleared totally and we could see across the bay to Anglesey. We leant on the fence and looked at the view. I pointed at a heron standing at the edge of the sea.

"I love the way they stand so still." Occasionally we could see him moving his head, his beak ever ready to spear any fish that came his way.

"You know, Ali..." Bob began, "I wish you wouldn't correct me when I make mistakes. I don't like it. I don't like it at all."

"I'm sorry Bobby. I really didn't mean to upset you. I am sorry."

"I can't help this bloody speech thing, this aphasia."

"I know."

"The trouble is you don't know."

"Well I try my best to understand."

"I know it's getting worse and I hate it."

"Do you think you should try to talk to the doctor about it?"

"No. I shall fight it myself."

I knew there was no point in arguing with him. He had his own way of dealing with life and its problems and I respected his independence. I pushed my worries away and got on with life.

In February 2004 I was ill with shingles, and Bob was a wonderful carer and did all the shopping and cleaning and cooking and made a good job of telling my clients why I wasn't coming to do their feet.

In May I became a grandmother again. Kira had a lovely little girl called Rosy. Around about the same time Bob and I built a polytunnel in the garden and one of my patients gave me an old hen coop so we bought 5 hens and put up a hen run. Bob went out walking with me on the mountains again though he did submit to using a walking pole to take the pressure off his knee. Life was pretty good and I very rarely worried about him. He sometimes mentioned that he wasn't remembering things so well. He was sometimes quite moody or angry with himself when he forgot things.

I noticed that he rarely read heavy books on philosophy and psychology now. He was busy reading all Shirley MacLaine's novels and when I had time I enjoyed reading them too. At night, when I was tired he loved to read out loud to me. He took great delight in reading the Pooh Bear books and was brilliant at putting on all the different voices. I teased Bob that he was Pooh when he was happy (and like Pooh he loved honey) but much more like Eeyore when he was moody. Bob said that if he was like Pooh then I was like Piglet!

"But I'm not as mucky as piglet!" I giggled.

***

In September we went on holiday to Cornwall in our new little car, an Aixam which Bob could drive with his old fashioned motorcycle licence. He was a good driver but had never taken a car driving test so it was the perfect solution. It didn't go very fast but on a run it did 90 miles to the gallon and we loved it. We decided to stop several times on the way, camping and staying in B & Bs. It was so nice not to have to do all the driving but our Aixam was very slow on hills. She would chug along quite nicely at 50mph on the flat roads and downhill with a tail wind, she might even reach 60mph. However, on narrow roads and going uphill I could almost see the steam coming out of the ears of drivers behind us as we happily chugged away up at 15mph!

While we were in Cornwall I celebrated my birthday in style with our old friends and relatives at a Thai restaurant in Penzance. It was a very happy evening and a great way to finish a wonderful holiday of walking on the moors and along the coast and just mooching about visiting old friends for chats and cups of tea. One day we went to see the Eden project with Alexis. I think it must be the biggest greenhouse in the world. It was very impressive!

***

Back in Wales I felt a bit down, torn between these two places I love. My mood wasn't helped by the weather which was wet and windy almost every day. But I also felt sad because Kira and Ariel were definitely going to Spain to live. In some ways I was happy for them. I could go and visit them in that beautiful warm country. It was a new adventure for them. They were buying some land with the intention of setting up a 'Raw Food Community' along with another couple from Scandinavia. I didn't think existing on only raw food was a very good idea and also the land had no house on it. They planned to build yurts to live in and to rent out but they didn't have very much money and I found myself worrying. Rosy was still a baby and Amber and Jasper were still so little too... and Kira still seemed so emotionally vulnerable. I found myself wondering how much her heart was really in the project. It was really Ariel's dream. I was looking forward to seeing them before they left and I also planned with my ex, John to visit them after Christmas to see how they were getting on. However, Bob complained about them coming. It was unkind and uncharacteristic of him. He seemed very moody.

"Do they have to come?" he moaned.

"Yes." I felt exasperated. Why did he not understand that I wanted to see them before they left for Spain? I was going to miss them.

Kira and the family arrived three days later. I know they tended to be a bit messy and noisy but Bob got into a right state several times. He'd never found them easy but this time he just couldn't seem to cope at all. He'd always been so welcoming, despite his need to retreat into his 'cave' from time to time. He'd always been so good with the children and enjoyed playing silly games, like giving them rides in the wheelbarrow around the garden or making sandcastles on the beach or just sitting and reading them stories. This time I noticed more than ever how easily he seemed to forget words when he was stressed. I was really worried about him. Suddenly the speech problem was so much more noticeable but there were other things that worried me too.

It was hard to put my finger on it but he sometimes said or did odd things. For example, when we'd first got back from Cornwall, we'd cut all the long grass at the top of the garden and I had suggested we put it in the garage to dry out so it could be used for the hen's nesting boxes and Quack's hutch. He looked a bit puzzled and then said that surely it could stay outside as it had all summer to dry.

"But it's nearly October, Bobby!"

"Oh yes, silly me," he laughed.

After the family had left Bob bought me a 'Teach Yourself Spanish' book for when I went over to visit them. Maybe he felt guilty for being so grumpy, bless him. So often his answer to everything seemed to be to buy a book.

Bob and I had a quiet Christmas, very different from last year.

Over New Year I met up with my ex, John, and we went out to visit our family in Spain. We were both worried about them living in the middle of nowhere on a piece of land and in tents. As I had feared there was no money left to build the yurts and yurts are expensive. Ariel had all sorts of ideas and projects for making more money but that would take time. Meanwhile it was freezing during the night in the valley where the land was situated. Fortunately, they were all in good health and the children were enjoying the outdoor life. While John and I were there we made a campfire every night and roasted potatoes in the ashes – so much for their plans to live on a raw food diet! Before we left we gave them some money and bought them a pile of food and a new mobile phone, but there was no electricity on the land so the battery

Holger and Bob removing the old summer house

was soon flat. Once we were back in the UK we could not get through to them and nor could the Scandinavian family that was moving out to live with them there. It was all very worrying but I just had to get on with my own life and treat no news as good news.

***

By February 2005 I had even more people wanting my services as a chiropodist, and Bob was busy with Holger removing the old summer house and putting up a new shed in its place.

Meanwhile I had planned two trips. Firstly I decided on a short trip to the continent to see my two nieces and their families. I so wanted Bob to come with me. We would be going to Rome and could go to some real Italian opera... but he was adamant that he didn't want to come. He seemed very nervous at the thought of travelling so far away. He said he was frightened of flying. I said that the planes nowadays are so much better than the old fixed wing Dakotas that he'd flown in once or twice as a young man. I also said that flying was the safest way to travel. He was far more likely to die on his motorbike speeding around the lanes as he did. Nothing I said made any difference. He had made up his mind and that was that, so I went on my own. I had a wonderful time seeing my nieces and their families and wandering around two of the most beautiful cities in the world: Paris and Rome.

After my return I planned an even bigger trip to Nepal in the autumn. This time I didn't even bother to try to persuade Bob to come with me. I knew it would be pointless. It was to be a charity trek round Manaslu, the 8th highest peak. I had fallen in love with Nepal when I trekked there a few years ago and this time I would be doing something to help those wonderful people. The money would pay for more medical centres high in the mountains where the nearest hospital is several days' walk away. I threw myself into fundraising and ended up with a few thousand pounds for the charity, Community Action Nepal.

***

The Good Girl Guide

All your problems will be aired
for I am the good girl guide.
My motto is to be prepared,
and my arms are open wide.
I am the little Miss Helpful,
I go where I am needed.
My diary has become quite full.
My man feels superseded.
Three grandchildren and daughter,
they really must come first,
I'm confidante and carer,
so Bobby must come last.
Babysitting, I can do it.
Hungry for food, I can cook it.
Longing for eggs. My hens are laying.
Hoping for games. I am playing.
Needing to stick something.
Well I've got the glue!
And so it is my darling,
that I have no time for you.

In March Kira came home. She had had enough of trying to survive in a freezing tent with three small children to look after and she and Ariel had split up. Ariel went with Jasper to London to work as a chef and Kira and the girls went to live with friends in Lancashire. It was all so sad and horrible and any spare time I had I was rushing around trying to do what mothers do, just trying to help. Poor Bob was very patient but I know he found it hard. He didn't have much of a look in when it came to us spending time together. I wrote a ditty for Bob.

***

I spent a lot of my spare time during April and May trying to help Kira and Ariel and the children. There didn't seem to be much hope of them all getting back together again but at some point Jasper went back to live with his mother and sisters and they moved down to Cornwall to a house that my ex, John, found for them.

After May, Bob and I had more time together and we went out a lot, walking on the mountains and when the weather was warm and I got back from work in time, we would regularly go down to Llyn Nantlle with a flask of tea and buns. I'd leave him sitting on the picnic mat while I swam halfway across the lake and back. I'd have liked to have swum further, but he would get anxious, not being much of a swimmer himself and I'd look back to see him watching me through the binoculars to make sure I wasn't drowning, I supposed. So I would return, get dressed and enjoy the hot tea and bun.

One day I returned from my afternoon swim to find a very flustered Bob. He had just witnessed an extremely attractive tall blonde girl strip off right in front of him and dive naked into the lake. His eyes, glued to her disappearing form, were sticking out on stalks and probably other things too.

"S ...Sorry" he stuttered, "I think she must be Swedish".

I just fell about laughing.

"It's okay my love. You are allowed to find other women attractive." I giggled.

I'd noticed recently how easily he became anxious. I had always been a bit of a tomboy. I didn't get scared easily. I was very confident in the water and also very confident with heights. In the past Bob would not have worried about my long swims or about me shinning up onto the roof to fix a loose slate or kneeling for hours on the garage roof painting it with 'Roofer's Mate' to try and stop the leaks. I always enjoyed heights and in the past, when Bob said he wanted to do these jobs I pointed out that I was 9 years younger, lighter on my feet and very agile. He was more likely to break more slates than mend them. Recently though, I tended to do these jobs when he was out, otherwise he'd be hovering around me and fussing and would become very moody if I didn't appreciate that he was only trying to look after me.

A year ago, before this tendency of Bob's to become so anxious, I wrote a poem about one particular time when I did swim to the other side of the lake.

Llyn

Across the lake I can hear the bleat of a sheep

calling its wayward lamb to come home

and further on the clankety clank of an aged jeep.

Here the banks are thick with moss and yellow buttercup,

two delicate, blue damselflies couple

and a swallow diving low after midges swoops up.

My lover's toes and then his feet dip in and wriggle,

scaring the tiny trout into darting away.

He backs off while I stagger with bare feet over gravel

shouting, "chicken, yer landlubber!
Get urn off, come on in!
Yer a scaredy-cat, get in yer bugger!"

Wading in, waving arms with an "Ooh ahh and eeeh!"
My legs, my crotch, my belly and "Bloody hell it's cold!"
I splash myself all over and yell "Whoopee!"

Sparkling droplets of water are splashing up high,
as I kick across the lake swimming breaststroke,
then backstroke so I can gaze up at the sky.

I am a fusion of natural at-oneness
with the lake and the mountains around me,
playing and laughing and swirling in coolness.

In a heaven of movement my legs tangle weeds
where the trees reach their roots down into the water
and a shy little moorhen scurries into the reeds.

While I sit on the bank the sky's suddenly black
I hurry my swimming, snorting and spitting.
The waves bumping at me, pushing me back.

Then I gulp down hot coffee, rub my shivering skin
while he laughs "so who's the daft bugger now?"
But I smile, for I know and he doesn't - what fun it has been.

I suppose like all couples we had good times and bad. We were both strong characters and stubborn with it, so although we both hated to fall out with each other, when we did, the sparks would really fly. Usually the argument would end with Bob saying angrily,

"I'm going!"

I would reply, "Well you know where the door is!"

At that he would grab his coat and march out. After hours I would think to myself, "I hope he's coming back..."

He always did, and we would hug and each say we were sorry, and then we would talk about why we'd argued in the first place. We both found this process helpful. Bob was not afraid to discuss his feelings like so many men are. Rows that ended like this often helped us to understand each other better and brought us closer. Sometimes he would stall an argument by looking at me severely and saying, "We need to talk!". Then I would feel as if I was a badly behaved child as he would proceed to give me a lecture on consideration for others! But, to be fair, he was generally ready to listen to my side of the story too.

***

We had lots of very happy, loving and fun times together just enjoying each other's company. We enjoyed time with other people too. We had made some good friends up here in Wales and during June we also had some wonderful days with old friends who came up to stay with us. We took them up into the mountains and we visited a couple of castles and also went to a concert.

At the end of June, I wrote in my diary:

"Bob had a lovely birthday today. We went out with friends to the Caban café and had a delicious lunch and then had a walk. I feel happy that we have good friends in Wales now and although I still miss Cornwall at times, I love it here in the mountains and we have got to know some wonderful people who we can both really talk to."

Reading this now, how I wish things could have gone on like this for the rest of our lives. I may have been concerned about Bob's memory and loss of words, but most of the time it didn't seem so very bad. Within a few weeks, however, Bob was suddenly a lot more forgetful. I began seriously worrying about being away for a month in Nepal. He began to get in a flurry sometimes when answering the phone. He stuttered and forgot words more and more and if I was out and one of my patients phoned for an appointment, he would often forget to tell me. I felt I couldn't rely on him anymore. If I gave him a list of things I needed in Caernarfon when he was going shopping and I was working, he would sometimes only remember one or two things and forget the rest. I tried to be very patient. He was too proud to confess to his difficulties. If I mentioned that he had forgotten something he would be cross and moody and snap at me that there was nothing the matter with his memory and that I had just forgotten to ask him to get those things. He'd been moody in the past but it was never like this.

One day I was out shopping and met two women collecting for the Alzheimer's Society outside Tesco's. As I put some coins in their box I asked them what the difference was between dementia and Alzheimer's. They told me that Alzheimer's was a type of dementia, the most common type, but that there were other types.

"Only... I think my friend may have a type of dementia. I try not to worry about it but it does seem to be getting a lot worse. Sometimes he seems fine but other times..."

They were lovely kind ladies and we stood there for a while talking. It was the first time I'd really voiced my fears to anyone and it all came pouring out to two total strangers. They told me that if I could persuade Bob to see the doctor he could do a few simple tests. Then if he thought Bob might have dementia, he could go to the Memory Clinic to see a specialist. When I arrived home from Tesco's I tried to think up a plan. I needed some sort of strategy. Bob hated going to the doctor and really hated hospitals. But he was booked in to see the doctor for a check up on his knee. Maybe we could somehow combine the two...

A few days later, I went to see the doctor myself. My IBS had been a bit worse so I used that as an excuse. Really I wanted to discuss Bob's problem with the doctor. Our surgery was one of the good old-fashioned types where you could just arrive in the morning with no appointment and wait in the queue. I got there early but there were still six others ahead of me. It gave me time to sit and think and jot down a few questions I needed to ask.

The doctor was wonderfully understanding of my worries which made me almost cry with relief. He asked me questions such as when did I first notice that Bob was forgetting words? How well was he able to manage his own affairs, such as money? Did he have trouble remembering things that had happened recently? He said that I should come with Bob if possible, so we went in together about ten days later. Amazingly, Bob had agreed to have a memory test *and* have his knee checked. Maybe, I thought, he was beginning to accept that he had a problem remembering words and other things.

When we visited the doctor I remember Bob being given a series of tests. He had to draw the numbers in the correct place on a clock face. Bob did that one okay. Then the doctor gave him the name and address of a fictitious person that he had to remember while he asked him other questions such as, 'What is the name of our prime minister and what is today's date?' Bob stumbled over words and he managed to answer some questions but he really did struggle with a lot of the questions and at the end he couldn't remember the fictitious person's name and address apart from his first name.

"John," he said with a look of relief on his face.

So the doctor confirmed that Bob had a memory problem and arranged for him to see a specialist at Bangor hospital.

At the beginning of August we went together to see the specialist, Doctor Kurian, at the hospital. At first Bob was happy to do the tests which proved he definitely had a big problem. His speech was very halting. It always was worse when he was nervous. He realised that he was performing very badly which made his speech even worse still. Bob was a very proud man. He had always been proud of his abilities and his memory. It must have been so hard for him to acknowledge that these abilities were fading.

Doctor Kurian asked Bob about head injuries. Bob said no, he hadn't had any head injuries. I interjected here. I told the doctor that Bob had often banged the front of his head on things. He had hit his head on low door lintels countless times. He was a very clumsy man. I also told the doctor that his speech problem started after that blinding headache he'd had when we were moving to Wales and that I thought it may have been a slight stroke. Doctor Kurian more or less told me to shut up at this point, politely of course, but I found it very hard. He said that Bob might be suffering from a type of vascular dementia but he would need to have a CT scan to confirm this. Bob got very uptight. "I'm not having any medical interference!" He looked furious and refused to cooperate any further with the doctor.

So Doctor Kurian said we could leave the CT scan for now but that he was going to arrange for Bob to have a Memory Clinic nurse visit him at home. Bob seemed happy with that.

A couple of weeks later I wrote in my diary:

"We're in Caernarfon... I'm sitting on a bench on the Maes waiting for Bob. I think he may have forgotten me. He's just looking for another Bryn Terfel CD in the Welsh shop nearby. It's a lovely day and I went out very early for a four hour walk as I've got to keep fit in readiness for the Nepal trip in October. I got back by 11 a.m. in time for the Memory Clinic nurse. She's called Bethan and seems ever so nice. Bob got on really well with her. I do hope it all helps. I worry sometimes that he won't cope when I go to Nepal but I'm trying to set everything in place so that he should be okay. He's always been great at looking after everything before but...

First of all, I need to contact all my patients and tell them not to ring me while I'm away. Bob is not coping with phone calls very well. Secondly, I need to talk to all our wonderful neighbours and friends and ask them to look out for him and call in from time to time. Thirdly, I need to leave him a few lists and instructions. Fourthly, I need to make sure there is plenty of oil for the central heating, plenty of hen food and plenty of cat food. He still seems to be pretty good at getting the day to day shopping done, feeding the hens and Quack and Chess. He's always good at keeping everything shipshape and it's only really things that are out of the ordinary... so a list of important phone numbers by the phone might be good."

***

Looking back I am surprised that I didn't cancel my trip to Nepal. I know I lay awake worrying myself sick but I also remember Bob being keen for me to go. He admired my ability to go off and travel in the high mountains on the other side of the world. He told everyone that he was proud of me and he insisted he would be able to cope.

When I couldn't sleep I would get up and write lists and notes and paste them on the cupboards to aid his memory. He complained about these lists but I pretended that the lists were for me as well.

"I'm getting forgetful too." I lied.

The Memory Clinic lady, Bethan, came to visit Bob about every couple of weeks. Bob said he really liked Bethan. She suggested various games to help his memory, but the only game he really liked playing was chess and the last time he'd played it with one of the neighbours, he became quite upset at how badly he played. He used to beat almost everyone at the game.

I was useless at chess so I would play the game with him sometimes. He could still easily beat me.

On 3rd October I left for Nepal after saying a fond farewell to my Bobby. I called in on friends and neighbours and also said goodbye to Chess and Quack and the garden. My trek around Manaslu was a very eventful journey. It would make another long story which maybe I will write one day but not here.

On my return from Nepal, four weeks later, the one thing I did feel so strongly was how kind and loving and special Bob was to me. Despite his memory problems he had coped so well and I was so pleased and relieved that he didn't seem any worse. We were both such free spirits and didn't want to be dependent on each other. I thought this time away from each other had shown that we could still be free spirits, hopefully for a good while longer.

I wasn't well during the last few days in Nepal. I was sick once and then had a constant feeling of nausea. As soon as I returned I had a queue of patients desperately needing their feet seeing to, so I was working flat out despite getting up half the night with the runs. I was losing weight fast and rather dramatically so in the end I went to the doctor.

It turned out I had *giardia*... a parasitic thing in your gut which I'd obviously picked up in Nepal. The doctor gave me the wrong medication twice and by Christmas Eve I was two stone lighter than normal and very weak. Eventually, I got the right medication and slowly recovered over the next two or three months.

***

In early December, Kira came to stay with all three children. She was behaving very oddly. Once again I was worried about her mental state. Then she went down with an almighty dose of flu. She seemed to be losing it both mentally and physically. She asked if Bob and I would look after Amber and Jasper for an indefinite period but I said I could not do it. I was feeling very weak with the giardia and Bob had dementia. In the end I took the two children down as far as Somerset and handed them over to Ariel's parents... Ariel was living with them and I thought that maybe the children would be better off with their father, for the time being. It felt like an awful decision to be making.

The journey to Somerset was pure hell as I was so weak with the *giardia*, and also so sick at heart at Kira's mental state.

The journey nearly finished me off. When I got home after driving for about 8 hours I was crying with pain and exhaustion. My dear Bobby held me with his big warm healing hands for a long time that night and I gradually relaxed and the pain and exhaustion subsided. I felt such warmth and healing coming from Bob's hands. He sometimes said that perhaps he should have done something with this natural ability; maybe massage or healing, but he never did.

Kira went back down to Cornwall just before Christmas with Rosy and then Bob and I just collapsed into each other's arms with relief at the much needed peace and quiet. Bobby looked after me in his wonderful gentle way until I was recovered but for a long time after I was very weak and thin and my body felt so sensitive to everything and there seemed to be so many things I just couldn't eat. He had to do so much for me and he managed really well despite his forgetfulness. Sometimes though I would have reminded him about something a bit too much or with an edge in my voice and then we'd have a bit of a spat... he'd say I was talking down to him or treating him like a child. Then he would be very upset and anger would spill out. Doctor Kurian saw him at the beginning of February and again suggested that he should have a brain scan, but again he said "I don't want any medical interference! I'm going to fight this memory problem on my own." I knew that this was totally illogical but there was no point in arguing with him.

***

One night around about the end of February I had a really humbling experience. I had never been so upset and angry with Bob before. It all started when I found that he had left the stove open at the bottom and the whole thing was red hot and roaring.

I had asked him to please stay with it for a minute or two and then close it up but he'd forgotten. He flared up at me when I sounded a bit cross.

"Stop talking to me as if I was a child!"

Then he started on about money and how he was unhappy with what he gave me each month towards water, rates, electricity and food. He said it wasn't fair but then he couldn't remember what wasn't fair. He went and got out all the paperwork and I tried to go through it with him to show him how we share the cost of everything. Then he brought up the money he'd paid when we bought the little Aixam car between us. I explained that he'd been happy to share the cost of the car as he used it too... He went on and on and I tried to reassure him by reminding him that he has been able to save more than he ever did when he lived on his own in Penzance. He retorted that I was much better off. "But I work. I earn my money." This was ignored. He seemed convinced I was cheating him and just went on and on. It was so unlike him and I just suddenly lost it, a great sweep of despair at what was happening to him welled up and overflowed and I cried and cried and cried some more and then I felt ashamed at getting so upset.

He did apologise when he saw me so upset and later he hugged me and said he loved me. He read me stories in bed. He loved reading to me. Eventually I fell asleep... I knew that I had to forgive him and accept him, but it was hard.

I was gradually getting better and was able to work more but I was still very weak and thin. During the time I'd been ill I didn't often feel like having sex. That side of our relationship had always been very important to us both. Over the months, Bob was very patient and understanding most of the time, but I know that it got us both down. Maybe this was a factor in his mood swings. Eventually I went to the doctor and was given some cream and that did help.

***

The hospital had been in touch about Bob's scan but he was still refusing to have it. They had been very nice about it at the Memory Clinic and were now coming to see him on the 14th of March. They said that without the scan he couldn't have a proper diagnosis. I decided to ask to sit in on the meeting but Bob was in a very bad mood on the day they came and they couldn't get anywhere with him.

"I am not having any medical interference!"

He dug his heels in and then refused all help of any sort. He said he had always got better in the past without help, so he didn't want their help anymore.

After they had left I tried not to think about it too much, otherwise I would have been totally overwhelmed with despair. I felt dumb and numb with sorrow as I packed my chiropody bag and went out to work. I could see a time coming when he would be so confused that I wouldn't be able to leave him and go to work. I tried not to think about that either. He refused to discuss his memory and speech problems with me anymore and went into total denial that he had a problem. I had read up about his type of dementia – the type that the doctor thought he had – and these mood swings and the sometimes totally illogical behaviour were typical.

In April I went down to Cornwall to visit all the family. Alexis was still living in Penzance and sometimes helped Kira by looking after Rosy for her. Kira did seem calmer and more her old self. Ariel was still looking after Amber and Jasper a lot of the time. I still wasn't well after the giardia but it was nice to see everyone. I worried how Bob would be while I was away so I didn't stay away too long.

In May I bought a little old camper van from a man down the road which I nicknamed Charlie. It was a bit of a rust bucket but it had a reconditioned engine and was going very cheap. It seemed like a great idea. Bob could no longer cope with camping in a tent so this was the next best thing. We had a couple of practice runs to a campsite near the Ogwen valley and then a long weekend down on the Llyn Peninsula near Aberdaron and it all went really well so I then I planned a trip to Cornwall for a couple of weeks.

Camping in Charlie, our campervan, was fun and we would be able to have a lovely two week holiday together but then suddenly Bob didn't want to go. He was in a very black and stubborn mood. "I'm not going to Cornwall." He announced. I was stunned. I never knew what would bring these moods on but they would hit me out of a clear blue sky and this one was the worst he'd ever had. I'd been so looking forward to our holiday in Cornwall and I'd thought Bob had too. I really didn't want to leave him on his own for too long but I said "Okay, perhaps I will go on my own".

He then talked about how he felt unhappy in our relationship and we then had a long and serious discussion about splitting up. I told him that I too sometimes felt like leaving him. I said that more and more there was no joy in our relationship. I told him that I was finding him difficult. One minute he wanted to do something and then the next he didn't.

I told him, "Your refusal to see the Memory Clinic people anymore makes me feel so very alone. Your refusal to have a simple CT scan makes no sense at all. You can't fight this on your own. You need all the help you can get! And I need help and support too. I can't help you all on my own!"

I often thought about the people with dementia in the old people's homes where I worked doing my chiropody and it was very difficult not to look ahead and dread what might happen to him. I knew I was selfish at times. I knew I would sometimes say unkind or slightly sarcastic things when I was tired and he was denying that he had forgotten something.

I told him, "It would help me if I could talk to you about how forgetful you are but you so easily take offence if I happen to mention you've forgotten something. I still love you but it's hard to help you because you are, and always have been, so proudly independent."

With a heavy heart, I suggested that perhaps I should sell the house so we could live apart. He said he was frightened to be "on the road again". I said that I would not do that to him. I would buy a small house for him and another small house nearby, for me.

I thought to myself, "Maybe we have come to the end of this particular road. I just don't know anymore... or maybe I should be prepared to cut back on my work. Then I could be there for him more... would that help? I really don't know."

Bob and the little Aixam car

Bob and Ali sharing a family meal

Chapter 4

The Beginning of Acceptance

After our conversation about splitting up, we both withdrew to our separate parts of the house. We gave each other space to think and feel our way through to the heart of the matter. I don't know quite what Bob thought and felt. He immersed himself in his music and went out a lot on his motorbike. When I wasn't working on people's feet, I thought the problems through. I felt shaken and heartbroken at the thought of us splitting up. I think Bob did too but I realised that I had been far too bossy recently. Bob needed to feel in charge of his life but with him getting more and more forgetful it was hard for me to stand back and let him make his own decisions. I realised I had hurt his pride by taking charge too often and that his independent free spirit must be struggling with his need to ask me for help. He was having a gigantic struggle with his masculine pride. Here was a proud and very independent person who now had to ask for help or if not in reality actually asking, realising he really needed to ask. I would have to learn to hold back and be more patient. In a way I would have to be wily if I wanted him to be happy with our relationship and if I wanted him to come to Cornwall. I decided to give him all the space he needed.

After a couple of days he came back into my side of the house and started cutting up vegetables.

"Would you like a veggie curry?" he asked.

"Oh, yes please, that would be lovely."

He looked at me and smiled, his blue eyes looked into mine with so much feeling that I just melted and gave him a big hug.

"I do love you, you know."

"And I love you."

We stood holding each other and then holding hands we wandered up the stairs. The veggie curry was put on hold for an hour or so.

***

Over the decision to go on holiday to Cornwall, Bob and I compromised. We agreed that half our holiday would be spent in Cornwall and half in Wales.

We drove slowly to Cornwall through the beautiful hills of mid Wales and camped the first two nights near the Wye valley. The next day we arrived in West Cornwall. The family came round to the campsite to greet us: Alexis, Kira, Jasper, Amber and Rosy. What a lovely surprise! I was very, very tired and felt as though I was going down with a cold... oh dear.

Our holiday was hard at times particularly as I did go down with a bad cold and probably kept Bob awake with my cough. Every night he would lumber out of his sleeping bag to pee and nearly knock the pee bucket over. Most mornings, when Bob woke up, he would say he wanted to go back home *now*, in a persistent childlike way. Then I would say that I really didn't feel well enough to do a long drive just yet, so could we leave in a day or so, please?

Then during the day, he would find that he was enjoying himself. We had fun walking along the cliffs and on the moors, the old walks we used to do before we moved. We spent time meeting up with the family and a few old acquaintances like his friend Jan and he would forget about wanting to go back home.

I could have done without the cough and cold but it did have its advantages! It meant that we stayed in Cornwall for a little longer than planned. On the way home, we camped near Cadair Idris and had a lovely day out. It was extremely hot weather and we spent time dipping our feet in a lake. We never reached the top but as we both agreed, it is the journey that counts, not arriving at a destination.

Bob was becoming more difficult, more moody, stumbling over words, stumbling through his days, losing things... his glasses, his purse, his keys. He would get himself into an angry mood because he knew he was making all these mistakes but didn't seem to be able to control the situation and it frightened him at times. I could see the fear in his eyes but he was too proud and too bravely stubborn to admit to his fears. When we did talk about it he was still adamant.

"I'm going to fight this myself!"

I was sure, as far as I could be, from reading things up on the internet that he had vascular dementia and not Alzheimer's. People with Alzheimer's lose their short term memory and do not have such mood swings. One thing I noticed was that he always seemed a bit better when there were other people with him. It was as if he made an extra effort to be as much like he used to be when there were other people around to observe him. This was good in a way but it did mean that most people probably thought I was exaggerating about how bad he could be. Friends and relations would make light of what was happening to Bob and say things like, "He doesn't seem too bad". Or "We all become forgetful as we get older." I'm sure they meant well. But I remember that this made me feel a bit lost for words and alone. It would have been so much easier if he had something obvious, like a broken leg or cancer even, not that I would have wished Bob to have either of those. But at least people aren't afraid to talk about cancer or broken legs quite so much. I tried to cheer myself up by telling myself that there were many, many people out there with far worse problems.

During July, I became extremely worried about Bob's ability to write. He suddenly had great difficulty writing a cheque out. In the end I had to help him before he screwed up half the cheque book with failed attempts. He blamed his glasses. He said he couldn't see where the faint lines on the cheque were, but the lines were not particularly faint and I knew, and probably he knew, that this was not the problem. I did suggest that he have another eye test. He hadn't had one for a while. I also suggested, rather tentatively, that he practice writing things down to keep up his skills.

"You have such beautiful handwriting and you could write that recipe book that you've often talked about."

With a bit of encouragement, he did do a little writing and reading regularly.

"It will help you to fight this memory thing," I said, but it really had shaken me to realise that he, who had once been so erudite, so clever, was forgetting how to write and read. My mind started to run ahead. How should I deal with this new problem? Would it get to the point when I would not be able to leave him on his own at all? At the moment he was still so independent especially with things that he did regularly. He never seemed to have problems with buying and cooking food. He could drive the car and his motorbike perfectly safely. He might be forgetful but he never forgot to feed Chess and Quack and the hens. He loved looking after our various 'creatures' as he liked call them. But he was getting worse. There was no doubt about it. I thought to myself, "I need to spend time with my family too. Maybe we should move back to Cornwall so I will be near them... but then we both love it up here in the mountains and we have made new friends and we have such good neighbours. Should we move somewhere smaller maybe... somewhere easier to manage?"

There were times when I couldn't sleep for worrying. Anything out of the ordinary would faze Bob. One day we had problems with our electricity. The trip switch kept tripping. He became very agitated about it. I managed to persuade him not to worry while I turned everything off. Then I turned everything on, one appliance by one until the trip switch went off again.

"It's that old electric heater that's causing the problem. We'd better get rid of it."

In the past Bob would have had no difficulty dealing with these sorts of problems. Another day soon after this, the electricity was off completely as there were repairs to be done in our area. I reminded Bob that this was going to happen but he had forgotten and I returned from work to a confused and agitated Bob who complained that there was something wrong with the bloody electricity again! Fortunately the electricity came on soon after that and we settled down to our evening meal and some soothing classical music on the CD player. Later in the evening, after we'd washed up and put the hens and Quack to bed we listened to the news. It was all about the war raging in the Middle East. Thinking about that made our problems seem very small.

During August, Bob and I went to the Faenol festival with Gillian and Holger again. Bryn Terfel was on top form and so was the tenor from Mexico... I have forgotten his name, but their singing was wonderful and the music sang in my head for days afterwards. Both Bob and I love music, especially live music, so it lifted our spirits.

With Bob becoming more difficult and forgetful, I decided to try and sell my chiropody practice. I put an advert in the Chiropody magazine and a lady called Ann phoned to say she was interested. I decided that if it didn't sell I would just have to really cut back. I worried about money a little but I knew I would manage. I would have my old age pension in September when l would be sixty.

At the beginning of September I began to take Bob out to work with me more often. He could make himself useful by carrying my chiropody cases and I checked with my patients to make sure they didn't mind. One particular day I wrote in my diary.

"Yesterday was wet and windy and Bob came with me to my patients. I have taken to asking if he'd like to come and pretend to need his help but really I just don't like leaving at home all day on his own. We met a fallen tree on the narrow lane to my first patient, Cemlyn, and had to turn back. Then we went to see some other patients in Caernarfon and did some shopping. Bob pottered around the charity shops and bought another book. He was thrilled with his acquisition. It was a book called "The Elephant Man," and he's always wanted to read this book because he's fairly sure that the doctor who looked after the Elephant Man was an ancestor of his. I wonder if he will manage to read it or whether it will just sit on his book shelves like so many other books he has bought recently. It was better weather in the afternoon and the fallen tree had been removed so I finally managed to get to do Cemlyn's feet. Later, we walked over to Gillian's with eggs and

some bread for Jim, her Dad. We stopped for a cup of tea and a slice of Gillian's delicious cake and Bob chatted to Jim about music. Jim used to play the drums in a band, so his taste in music is rather different from Bob's. We did some blackberrying on the way home. I left Bob picking some more blackberries and went ahead to make a blackberry and apple crumble and a salad and Spanish omelette for tea. Most of our meals are our own produce from the garden at the moment."

More and more I noticed that Bob would start things and then stop and then start again. I noticed that when he sat to read a book now he would often get stuck, sometimes reading the same page over and over. If he was writing something down he would sometimes write the same line twice or even three times. I just observed and said nothing. Another thing that seemed to be happening more and more was that he had taken to waking up in the middle of the night and thinking it was time to get up. Around this time I wrote:

"He woke me at 3 a.m. this morning, thinking it was time to get up so I shall probably have to sleep in the other room tonight to catch up. I will miss him next to me though. I feel very gentle towards him, accepting more his inability to find words and his forgetfulness. I wish... no, I shall not wish, for things are as they are. If I start to go down the track of wishing he was well I will just end up with a feeling of despair."

My diary entries at this time were full of this problem of him waking up.

"I'm finding Bob's behaviour very wearing. I'm not getting as much sleep as I need. He seems to be more and more restless and often wakes me up in the middle of the night. I need to be able to fully concentrate when I'm doing my job. I can't be using sharp instruments on old people's feet if I feel half asleep with tiredness." And a week or so later I wrote: *"Bob seems to want his own space so I'm in the other bedroom. We haven't been getting on too well and had a spat over nothing. I'm not a bad person but I'm not good either. In the morning Bob woke me at 6:30 saying that he didn't want to wake me but he wanted to know what the time was."*

Over the next month or so this pattern of waking up and not knowing what the time was made me realise that the root cause was that he was losing the ability to tell the time. I bought a large kitchen clock and put it on the wall facing his bed. I hoped that this might help but at first it only seemed to annoy him.

"What are you putting that up there for?"

"Well you often seem to be asking me what the time is, so I thought this might be easier for you to read."

"You don't need to patronise me!" he grumped at me.

"I'm not Bob, but I need my sleep and you need yours. I'm only trying to help."

The clock stayed on the wall but it didn't help the situation.

A few weeks later I wrote in my diary:

"Bob woke me at 3:30 a.m. asking what the time was. I looked at the clock and told him that it was 3:30.

"Oh yes" he said. "So it is."

I felt cross at being woken and said that he probably would have read the time wrong anyway. It was so unkind of me. It's obvious to me now that he is struggling to tell the time but I shouldn't have rubbed it in. I tried to excuse myself by saying that it didn't matter.

"Of course it matters," he muttered as he went off to the bathroom for a pee.

I felt so bad about it that I marched off to the other bedroom. I tried to sleep but couldn't. "I'm a right bitch," I told myself. "He can't help how he is." I came back to bed and said I was very sorry but I still couldn't sleep."

A few months later I even drew an arrow on the wall next to the 7 o'clock positions but nothing made any difference and he continued to wake up and ask what time it was. I was exhausted from lack of sleep. I took to sleeping in the other room more often.

However, there were ups in our life as well as downs. At the end of September I had my sixtieth birthday and Bob managed to make me a beautiful Dundee cake, my favourite! We invited a few friends and neighbours over and had a small 'Life begins at 60' party. I couldn't believe I was sixty. When I was young I thought sixty was old but I still felt so young inside.

At the beginning of October we went to a wonderful concert with Dafydd and his girlfriend Jenn. It was called 'The Devil's Violin'. The music and gypsy stories were magically interwoven and we both felt uplifted and spellbound by it.

Unfortunately, the chiropodist lady, Ann, decided not to take over my practice, so I had to write to all my clients and explain the situation. Most of my regulars already knew that Bob was not too well and were very understanding. I had a spare room in the house so I told them that if they could come to me that would be best, but also if they didn't live too far away, then I could keep them on. Otherwise they would have to find another chiropodist.

In mid-October I went up to Lancashire and stayed at Gillian's other house as Chorley is not far from the Aixam agent where I bought our little car. It was in need of a repair after Bob had pranged it and I wanted them to give it a thorough check up. I realised that there would come a time when Bob would have to give up driving but apart from this slight prang he still seemed to drive very well. However, his motorbike sometimes wouldn't start and I did begin to wonder whether he was doing something wrong or whether the bike really needed fixing – as he said it did. One of our neighbours, who used to run a motorcycle shop, examined the motorbike thoroughly and he said that there was nothing wrong with it as far as he could see.

***

Towards the end of October Kira phoned me in a terribly upset state. She was having so many problems, especially with Jasper, so I decided to go down to Cornwall for a short visit over the half term to see if I could help. I was exhausted before I even left Bangor station. My dear Bob was so anxious to get me to the train on time that he started getting up at 2 a.m. in the morning.

"What are you doing Bobby?"

He got back into bed and went back to sleep but I couldn't. After a while I crept into the other bedroom and read for a bit. I lay awake wondering if I'd remembered to have everything left so he wouldn't get himself into any pickles while I was away. I tried to think of everything. The bins were emptied, the car was full of fuel, and the fridge was full of food. Instructions were sellotaped to the mantelpiece. I didn't think I had forgotten anything.

The train left at 10 o'clock. Bobby stood on the platform waving goodbye. I blew him a kiss and I got out my diary and started to write:

The train is going along near the shoreline. I can see the Great Orme in the distance for a moment and then we are plunged into the dark by a short tunnel and now out again into the sunshine with yachts bobbing in the bay and then we arrive at Llandudno Junction where we stop. My eyes are starting to close. I'm so tired. I think I'll just have a nap. I don't change trains until Crewe."

It was dark by the time I arrived in Penzance and I was very tired. Alexis met me and drove me over to Kira's house. Kira fed us both on veggie casserole and we helped her put the children to bed. I could see how fragile and tired she was but I don't think she had any idea just how very tired I was too and it wouldn't have helped to tell her. At least I wouldn't have Bob waking me up half the night asking what the time was. I did hope he would be okay but I was too tired to worry and slept like a log every night.

Later on the journey I wrote this poem.

***

Life

Life is a challenge,
meet it.
A gift,
accept it.
A sorrow,
overcome it.
A duty,
perform it.
A game,
play it.
A song,
sing it.
A promise,
fulfill it.
A puzzle,
solve it.
Love,
enjoy it.
Beauty,
praise it.

A few days into my stay, I received some very sad news. I was playing with the children in the garden making an Eeyore house out of sticks when Kira called out from the house.

"Your phone is ringing!" It was Bob. I thought he was trying to tell me that our cat, Chess, was sick as he had been a bit unwell a few days ago, but no. Bob was in a terrible state and couldn't get his words out properly but he managed to tell me that he'd found Chess by the hedge and that he'd lost the use of his back legs. He'd probably been hit by a car. I talked to him calmly and told him to take Chess to the vet.

Later he phoned again. He'd lost his keys. I suggested various places and he wandered around holding the phone while I talked to him until he found them. Later he phoned again. Poor Chess had been put down. His spinal cord was broken. Bob told me that he held him in his arms while the vet gave the injection. He phoned again later. He had buried Chess in the garden. He sounded so upset. I wished I was home so I could comfort him but I was going to be at Kira's for a couple more days. Bob told me not to worry. He was okay, he said, so I took the children out swimming and they cheered me up.

A few days later I took the train home. I nearly missed it trying to do too many things for Kira and the children before I left. It had been lovely to spend time with them and it was also good to have a whole week of being able to sleep right through the night without being disturbed. However the evening before I left I had another shock.

I was busy packing for the journey home when my phone went. It was Bob.

"We've got problems," he said.

"I'm on the way to the station to pick you up and I can't get the lights to work on the little car."

"Bobby! I'm not coming home till tomorrow."

"Oh my God!"

"Where are you?"

"I'm down at the Ozanam Centre with Steve."

"Well put Steve on."

I talked to Steve and asked him to show Bob how to turn the lights on. I explained that Bob was getting more forgetful and thanked him profusely for helping.

Later Bob phoned from home. He told me that when he couldn't work the lights he'd driven all the way down the lane, nearly a mile in the dark with no lights. Thank God he didn't meet anything.

"It was a bit hairy," he said.

A bit bloody scary, I thought. I was upset.

"Please never do that again."

I suggested he practice turning the lights on and off so he didn't forget when he came to pick me up the next day.

Was the whole world going crazy? What with Kira and her problems and Bob and his dementia, I felt I was going slightly bonkers too.

When I got home the next day Bob solemnly walked with me up the garden to show me Chess's grave at the top. It was a massive affair for one admittedly fairly big cat with an enormous pile of stones on top. But then Bob had been a grave digger and Chess had been his special friend.

"That's a wonderful grave, Bobby."

I suggested we bought some cat nip and other plants that Chess might have liked and turn it into a sort of rockery grave.

***

After a hectic few days of washing clothes, doing people's feet, digging the garden and leaving everything in order, I was away again at the Welsh writer's centre, Ty Newydd, on a course I had booked ages ago. It was a wonderful few days of writing poetry but it all felt a bit mad, what with having the unplanned trip to Cornwall and Bob getting worse.

There was no mobile signal in the house so it wasn't until I went out for a walk that I found that Bob had been phoning me over and over again. I phoned him and he told me he'd forgotten where I was and thought I'd left him!

"I'd never leave you." I couldn't help crying and that made

Bob tell me off in his confused way. I felt so guilty that I'd gone away again when his forgetfulness was getting so much worse.

"It's just I can't start my motorbike."

He went into a long confusing explanation.

"Look my love, for now I should just get the bus and we'll sort your motorbike out when I'm home. I'm back on Friday..."

I phoned Andy and Deb to see if they could call in to check Bob was okay but they were out. I tried not to beat myself up for being away yet again. This course was important to me. I was planning on doing an M.A. in creative writing, starting after Christmas at Bangor University and the point of this short writing course at Ty Newydd was to help me regain some confidence in my ability to do creative writing. The tutors were excellent and despite my feelings of guilt I was glad I had gone to it. The M.A. would only involve being gone for a few hours every Tuesday afternoon and evening. Surely Bob could cope with that.

The next Sunday we went to the Quaker meeting for the first time for ages. People said they had missed us and it was good to see everyone. Later, after lunch, we went for a cycle ride though it was grey and spitting slightly. We were going up a tiny lane when Bob suddenly decided to stop and turn his bike upside down.

"Will you hold this little cap?"

Pump pump, jiggle jiggle. I started to giggle when he said, "Well that's hard".

"Don't be rude!" He giggled too.

Then, "Oh sod it," when I handed him the cap, "I can't get it on! Oh shit! Hold this!"

I leaned my bike against the wall and sat on a builder's bulk bag by the gate. There were dead leaves everywhere and I held the caps firmly in case I dropped them. After a gigantic struggle he finally managed to screw both the caps back in place.

Finally the bike was righted and wiped clean of dead leaves.

"Shall we go?"

More leaves rustled to the ground as we cycled on.

I pondered on this incident. Either Bob's dexterity was being affected by his condition or he was just getting more long sighted. I was not sure. Later, when we returned from the bike ride I met Andy and Deb, in the lane and found out why he'd been having a problem starting the motorbike. Apparently he had wheeled it round to them while I was away.

"Look, the thing won't start," he said as he pressed the horn which is next to the starter motor, "it just makes a silly tooting noise!"

Andy and Deb tried to keep a straight face and suggested he put the 'thing' back in the garage and catch the bus. Now there was another hurdle to jump over. I knew I really should try to persuade Bob to sell the motorbike. I was not looking forward to talking to him about it and I'm afraid I chickened out of doing so. He did so love going out on it... but if he couldn't even remember how to start it, goodness knows what might happen. And then there was the little car... he wanted to drive it but maybe he shouldn't go on his own any more. If only he would go back to the Memory Clinic or the doctor.

It was the end of November and Bob continued to regularly disturb my sleep. One evening I made the mistake of telling him I needed to make an early start the next day. So Bob woke me at 4:30 a.m. saying it was 6 a.m. I thanked him but said that I wouldn't get up just yet. I made a mental note not to say that I was planning on getting up early in future. I know he only wanted to be helpful.

Later that day, while I was out working, he went around to our neighbour, John, who helped him with a form he needed to fill in. Bless John; I was so grateful for kind neighbours.

Meanwhile I had been saying goodbye to many of my patients, especially the ones in the residential home that was furthest away.

I wrote a poem about one of the old ladies there who could not speak properly anymore.

Mai

She shouts at the carers, waves them away.
"She won't get dressed," they say.
But she's beautifully impish,
grins from ear to ear when she sees me.
"A chi, chi, chi," she waves her hands.
"Hello Mai, I've come to do your feet."
And while I trim her nails she pokes me.
"Look! Ch, ch, ch…"
She points to her clothes in the wardrobe.
" Look ch, ch, ch."
"Yes, you have some lovely clothes, Mai."
She is quietly smiling now and pokes me once more.
She points to the door.
"Er cu, cu, cu," she mimics fat cheeks and eating.
"Er bi bi bi." I know she's making fun
of the woman across the corridor
who's fat,
not like Mai but a body with no legs,
the wheelchair creaking,
eating, eating,
continuously.
The TV turned to blasting.
She laughs, "You are a scamp," I shake my head.
She laughs again, mimics again

the fat cheeks stuffed and eating.

We laugh as I rub her feet

and move to trim her fingernails.

This is harder; she wants to wave her hands.

I have to hold them still,

but soon I finish.

Now she can show me, like she always does,

the sepia photo of her husband.

A younger Mai standing beside him

dressed for their wedding.

Delicately Mai holds the golden frame

and kisses him through the glass.

I hold her hand then

pack my things to go.

She blows me a kiss as I say,

"Goodbye, Mai,"

And wave her a kiss too,

"Look ch ch ch! "

As I walk away.

Christmas was not far away and Bob spent all weekend trying to write a Christmas letter to his friend Ben. While he did that, I wrote most of our other Christmas cards and letters. He had a tremendous struggle writing this letter but was determined to do it. I wanted to help, but not too much. His struggle made me face once again the reality of his dementia, for what else could it be?

He finally wrote the letter to Ben, with as little of my help as possible, saying that he had some degree of memory loss. It was difficult for him to confess this to Ben, let alone write it, but he overcame his pride and bravely sent the letter off. I had thought he might not have had the courage.

I kept meaning to look up more things to do with dementia on the Internet but I just couldn't face it, so I kept putting it off. I was afraid of facing too many facts when he wouldn't go back to the doctor so I just tried to accept how he was and work with it as if it was normal. It was as if we were both playing a game of 'hide from the dementia'. We were like two people sitting in a boat with a hole in the bottom, letting the water in. It was as if we believed that if we ignored the hole and pretended that it didn't exist, it would somehow magically mend itself and disappear!

But there were times when I would lose patience with this pretence and then his 'pride' would make him erupt.

"Don't talk to me like I'm a child!"

"I want to deal with it in my own way!"

***

He saw his problem as mainly loss of speech. Sometimes his speech was fine but other times he just couldn't find the words. Sometimes our conversation was so incongruous. One day, for example, I said

"You are the most illogical of men."

"That's nice; I like to think I'm the most logical of men."

Did he mishear or misunderstand?

Another time I asked him if he had a ruler. He felt in his pocket and brought out a comb.

"Here you are." He did realise he'd made a mistake after a moment or two.

I tried not to say anything but I was not sure what to do. At least he had managed to write to Ben. That at least was a breakthrough.

***

We had a lovely Christmas meal with Gillian and Holger and a quiet New Year sitting by the fire watching the flames going up the chimney, while Bob read to me. I remember he was reading 'The No. 1 Ladies Detective Agency,' by Alexander MacCall Smith. He read very slowly, but he was still able to put plenty of expression into the different voices in the story. Sometimes I would fall asleep, soothed by the sound of his voice. I loved him reading to me and it was good for him to keep in practice, but he didn't like me falling asleep so I would try to pretend I hadn't. "I was just resting my eyes." I'd tell him.

Time marched on. I began to notice that Bob was starting to have more problems driving the little car but it didn't seem too serious. I remember one evening though, when we took a friend to a concert in Bangor cathedral. Bob insisted on driving there and nearly made a mistake that could have resulted in an accident. Before we set off home our friend asked me, "Please would you drive us home, Ali". She said it rather anxiously and I felt a pang of guilt at having allowed Bob to drive that evening. It was so difficult because I so wanted Bob to feel that he was normal. He wasn't facing the fact that he was no longer functioning normally so I didn't face up to it either, most of the time.

Having cut back on the number of patients I treated, I now had more time to spend with Bob. We had more time to sit together, listening to music in the evenings or even during the day when the weather was foul. We went out walking together more often too. I continued to encourage him to read and write so he didn't forget how and in the meantime I started doing the part time M.A. in creative writing. I really enjoyed it. I would sit by the fire in the evening writing a poem or a short story and would suggest to Bob that he could do some writing too.

"I'll do some later," he'd usually say though sometimes he would try to do a little.

I tried to look no further than each day, never knowing what mood he would be in. One good day was often followed by one awful one. On good days, Bob and I might meet up with friends or go to a concert or the cinema. We went to a drumming event one night to raise money for a village in Africa. That was great fun

One wonderful late afternoon I walked up to the quarry behind our house to watch the sun go down. Bob joined me and we walked together, enjoying the most beautiful sunset. It was like a wonderful gift from heaven. Snowdon was snow covered and went pink as the sun sank. There were so many different types of clouds all catching the light at different times and in different ways, showing up as grey and pink and orange and red while the sky went from blue to egg shell blue with a tinge of green. It was so amazing and we kept stopping and looking and gazing in wonder. Bob was regretting that he didn't have his camera but I think somehow that might have interfered with his enjoyment of this spectacle of light. It was growing dark when we arrived home. It was time to put the hens and Quack to bed, have a cup of tea and light the fire.

Other days might be difficult because we were both tired from Bob having a disturbed night or because he had lost his wallet or his glasses or sometimes just because he was in a bad black mood. Sometimes now he became so convinced that it was time to get up that he would start to get dressed at two in the morning. The kitchen clock that I had bought and stuck on the wall didn't seem to be much help, but I left it there.

***

At the beginning of February I went to my sister, Jenny, in London for a long weekend. I hadn't seen her for a long while and I was missing her. I decided I would phone Bob at least once a day to make sure he was alright. All went well while I was away but I was late back from London having missed a connection at Llandudno Junction and was a bit worried that arriving late might confuse Bob but I managed to contact him before he'd left home to pick me up. He had been fine while I was at Jenny's, though he'd hardly eaten anything... just fruit and bread and very little else. I asked him about it, but he said he was pleased because he'd lost weight. However, not bothering to cook for himself was not a good thing, especially if I decided to go away for longer.

The next day we woke up to snow and later in the morning, when the sun came out we built a snowman in the garden using the coal shovel. We played like big kids and had a snowball fight with our neighbours, Andy and Deb, and then invited them over for a hot cup of coffee. The next day we had even more snow and there was a howling gale. Poor Quack had her dish of food blown over. She ran behind her hutch quacking unhappily. It was so windy and foul I put her back inside her hutch and there she stayed until the afternoon when the wind had died back a bit. She went to her pond then, but that was frozen solid. All together she was not a happy old duck. The hens only laid one egg which was not surprising with such cold weather.

I'd arranged for our friend and will expert, John to help us do our wills. I thought he might not be able to come over with so much snow about, but he did. Bob's will was simple as he didn't have much except for the money in his bank which he wanted to leave to me. Mine was complex, as I owned the house but I wanted to make sure that he would be allowed to stay in it for the rest of his life even though the house would go to my children. We got Andy and Deb to witness everything though Bob didn't like the whole process and nearly threw a wobbly. I think he suddenly felt nervous that making a will would mean he'd be going to die soon for sure! Silly man, I thought, but then I've never been superstitious like that.

A few days later I helped Bob fill in a form so that his housing benefit could be paid straight into the bank. It had been difficult to persuade him but it would be so much safer than a cheque arriving in the post which he then had to take to the bank himself and pay in. I knew he liked to do things face to face, in the old-fashioned way, but as he became more forgetful there was always the worry that he would lose the cheque or just forget to pay it in. It was a relief to me to get these practicalities over the Will and his benefit sorted.

***

On February 14th Bob gave me two Valentine cards. He'd never given me even one before. It was a lovely thought... but then he got very upset because he couldn't write properly in either of them. I said it didn't matter and gave him a big hug.

"It's the thought that counts." I said brightly, and I really meant what I said. I felt so much in that moment that words were just inadequate. I saw Bob's brave and stubborn way of insisting he must fight this illness, every step of the way on his own. I saw his love for me shining out of his face and somehow my love for him seemed puny. His love for me was so unconditional.

"No," he said, suddenly sounding very determined.

"No. I think I'd better go back to the quack. I ...err... um... It's getting worse. This thing... it's like a hole in my head... I'm going to fight it but maybe I do need some help."

Suddenly he was realising just how bad his memory loss was. I could hardly believe what I had heard. He'd said, without any prompting from me, that he would go back to see the doctor. Had he really said that? I couldn't quite believe it but I wanted to believe it. There might not be much that could be done to help him, but at least the doctors would do what they could and at least he was coming around to accepting a situation, an illness that we both found so hard to accept. Life for so long, or so it seemed to me, had been about pretending that what was happening was just a bad dream. That sooner or later we would wake up and everything would be better. This was the beginning of acceptance.

This was the beginning of a different sort of fight. It wouldn't make the dementia go away. It wouldn't make the truth of the situation any better or any worse but at least now we could talk about it. Not talking about it and trying to pretend that everything was fine had been so hard. I gave my Bobby the most enormous hug.

"Thank you for saying that my love."

87

Bob making a snowman with the coal shovel

Chapter 5

Looking Back and Moving Forward

In the second half of February, Bob went back on his resolution to see the doctor. I had hoped so much that he would go to the doctor and I made the mistake of encouraging him once too often, so it probably seemed to him that I was nagging. I also made the mistake of mentioning once too often that he had forgotten something. I tried to understand his frustration and touchiness. I supposed that the difficult mood swings he had were connected to the dementia but I couldn't be sure. I so wanted some sort of certainty even if it was an awful certainty that he had vascular dementia for certain and that there was nothing that could be done. This continuing pretence that there was nothing very wrong with him, was for me the hardest thing. Perhaps for him it was better not to know and to keep pretending but I wasn't inside him.

Watching what was happening to him from the outside was agonising at times, like some sort of growing nightmare that I couldn't wake up from. The only respite I found was in trying to see the funny side of things. He was forgetting things more and more frequently and often getting into a muddle. For example, he would go up the garden to feed the hens leaving the bucket of feed in the porch.

"Bobby!" I called after him and waved the bucket.

He went out to fill the coal scuttle one evening and came back with it full of wood. I said nothing.. We needed wood for the fire too. Later when he was out of the room, I transferred the wood to the log basket and slipped out quietly to get the coal myself.

Another time he said he was going to make a casserole and when I went into the kitchen I found him cutting the onion up with the skin still on and putting the whole lot into the saucepan.

"We can't eat onion skin, Bobby," I said as I started to fish the skin out of the pan.

"Why not?"

"Well... I don't think it's very nice..."

This was seen as me trying to control him.

Another day when we were going shopping to Caernarfon we spent an hour looking for his glasses and his wallet.

"Have you put them in the car?" I asked.

"No, I haven't been out to the car," but after scouring the house I went out to the car and there they were.

Later that day when we arrived home I said, "Bobby, my love, please would you go to the doctor soon, like you said you would..."

He suddenly got very angry and said he was not going to see *any* doctor and that he was *not* going to be controlled by me telling him he'd forgotten something or other. I told him I was sick and depressed with pretending there was nothing the matter. I told him that I needed to say that I could see him getting gradually worse and I could no longer cope with pretending. I told him our relationship had always found its strength in being honest with each other!

And then we were very honest with each other – it was all quite harsh. I said that there were no answers and that he obviously had dementia of some sort and he needed to face it. I said I didn't know if I had the patience to be a good carer, but it might come to that. He said I was controlling and that I spent too much time on the phone talking to friends and family. In his anger he became quite erudite again. He said he wanted to be left alone and not to be organised at all.

"Okay," I said, and went upstairs with the phone to the other bedroom. I shouted down the stairs, "I shall phone up people as much as I like but upstairs where you can't hear me in future and I shall leave you, you bloody man, alone!"

I felt that he was actually being more controlling than me at times and we both hated to be controlled. But as helping him was seen as control, I would not help him either, not unless he really, really asked and asked or I saw him doing something dangerous!

Then I thought, "I hope he doesn't do anything dangerous. I do love him very much. I just don't want him to deny that there's a problem."

I suddenly felt better that we'd fallen out and spoken our minds. We hadn't been doing that enough.

A week or so later, Rosy, Kira and her new boyfriend, Brett, came to stay for a few days. Brett seemed a nice guy and they both seemed very happy. I hoped it would work out for them. Rosy was very good for Bobby. He enjoyed playing games with her and reading her stories. She accepted his slow, halting reading of the stories very happily and that was good. He so liked to read out loud. For a while his speech and his ability to think logically seemed a lot better though it might just have been the stimulus of having other people around and his enjoyment in playing children's games with Rosy.

In March we acquired a new little cat. We called her Heidi. She was a rescue cat and about four years old. She was pretty: white with tabby patches. I hoped she and Bob would get on. I thought it would be nice to have another 'creature' for Bob to look after but she was a bit timid and not at all like Chess. Bob was very protective towards her. She loved to climb trees and would then meow pitifully from high up in the branches. She was perfectly capable of coming down on her own but Bob would insist on going up the ladder to rescue her. He would come down with her clinging to his shoulder and all he got for his pains was a clawed shoulder!

***

It was about this time that Bob had an interesting conversation with one of my patients. Rob and his wife Patricia had been regulars of mine for some time and I would usually visit them in their home, but with Bob's problems increasing, they agreed to come to our house for treatment. Rob, who was ten years older than Bob, had told me that he'd been brought up in a children's home in Birmingham. He told me of the terrible time he'd had there and how it had scarred him for life, and then he told me it was called 'Father Hudson's.

I said, "That's the same one that Bob went to." Since then he'd always wanted to meet Bob so this was his opportunity.

After I'd done Rob's feet, Bob made everyone a cup of tea and then he and Rob went and sat in the sitting room so they could talk while I got on with Patricia's feet. Bob talked about their conversation later.

With the ten year age gap, they hadn't known each other at the home but many of their experiences were similar. The regular beatings were normal but they both suffered from nerves which led to bed wetting. If this happened, the nuns would get them up, beat them and make them wash their sheets there and then. Then the wet sheets would be put back on the bed and they would have to lie on them. How they didn't get pneumonia, goodness knows.

Bob was a tough lad and had found ways of escaping from the worst effects of the home, either by running away or hiding, but he knew that some boys were regularly sexually abused both by some of the priests but also by some of the other members of staff and Rob had suffered this abuse himself. Bob was a good listener and I could hear his sympathetic tones through the door. When they came back into the kitchen, Rob's eyes were red with tears.

"You shouldn't have been talking about that place."

"It always makes him cry." Patricia said, turning to me.

This meeting with Patricia and Rob brought back memories for me too. I lay awake that night remembering some of my first meetings with Bob when I was just a friend offering a listening ear to an obviously troubled man... and what conversations we'd had.

I remembered years ago when he'd told me of how one holiday the nuns had arranged for him to go to a farm on the Welsh borders to help the farmer. He couldn't remember how old he was but he can't have been more than ten or eleven. Perhaps the nuns saw it as some sort of work experience and Bob probably had said that he loved the outdoors. But the farmer saw it as a very different type of opportunity! He made Bob work very hard but after a few days he kept trying to touch Bob in an inappropriate way. Bob had seen enough at Father Hudson's to know what he had in mind, so he made his escape across the fields. Apparently the farmer leapt on his tractor and tried to recapture him. Bob ran and ran around the big field until he came to a gate, the farmer shouting threats and in hot pursuit. I remember Bob chuckling when he described the scene and how he climbed the gate and ran on and on. I remember admiring his ability to see the funny side of the situation.

Apparently, he then walked and hitched lifts all the way back to Birmingham and the relative safety of the family home.

I think, after this episode, his mother decided he'd be safer at home. He was sent to the local school for a while but the abuse that his mother received from his stepfather was still going on and he and his sister Betty and their step brother David would regularly run from the house to get out of the way of his fists.

Eventually, when Bob was about thirteen, he decided he couldn't stand it anymore and pinched someone's bike in order run away from home. He was stopped by the local policeman who knew about all the family's troubles and the result of this was that Bob was sent to Borstal, because, they told him he was 'in need of care and protection'.

He did manage to impress the Borstal authorities with his intelligence and good behaviour and was sent to college to do his 'O' and 'A' level exams and then went on to University College, London, to study law. However, sadly, his mother died and this upset him so much he didn't finish his degree. He left to live one day at a time. He would take a job here, a job there, travel on to another town, another place, never settling down.

So Bob had done a lot of running away in his life but it seemed that now he no longer wanted to run away – apart from the reality of his dementia. He had found his home at last in this beautiful part of Wales but now it was me who felt like running away. I dreamt over and over of going on a 'round the world' trip. I had had a letter from an old friend who was living in Thailand and married to a lovely Thai girl. The letter said he was having all of his friends over for his sixtieth birthday and would I like to come?

I'd have loved to. I dreamt over and over again of getting a 'round the world' ticket and going to New Zealand and India as well as Thailand. I did so want to travel to these places and other places too, so, so much but I knew that I couldn't leave Bob for that long.

Then my friend Helen asked if I'd like to go to China with her next April. I said I'd love to but with Bob and his dementia? I pondered and pondered. Maybe, I thought to myself, maybe I *could* go to China. We'd only be gone for just over two weeks. I decided – sod it – I would say yes to her proposal. If Bob could no longer manage without me for that long, then I would arrange for someone to look after him , and to be honest, I needed something to look forward to. I was not a natural carer. I knew I needed the thought of this trip to lift my spirits. I wanted to escape from this horrible thing that was happening to Bob. I was the one who wanted to run away now.

I shared my problems with Gillian quite often and one day Bob told me that Gillian had been up to the house while I was out at work and had had a chat with him about going to see the doctor. He seemed very impressed with her understanding of his situation and although he said he still wouldn't have a scan on his brain he said he *was* thinking of going back to see the doctor. He said that he'd admitted to Gillian that he tended to procrastinate. Well, that was putting it mildly! Actually I knew she'd been talking to him and had been trying to persuade him to go back to the Memory Clinic because she'd told me. I was so grateful for her help but Bob still didn't go to the doctor and I really wasn't coping very well.

More and more he seemed to be like a life's test that I was failing miserably on. More and more I felt that I didn't even want to cope. I knew that with the way things were, I was probably going to have to cut back on my work even more and I resented that. I enjoyed my job. I enjoyed the financial independence it gave me but Bob was wearing me out. Nearly every night he would wake me up at least once and often he would start getting washed and dressed at 2 or 3 or 4 a.m. and then during the day there would be other muddles to sort out.

I remember one day I asked him to feed Quack and Heidi, the cat, when we got back home in the afternoon. I got on with the cooking and then found he had given Quack the cat food and Heidi the duck food! Quack, being the guzzler she was, ate it all up but poor Heidi... It seemed funny and we had a good laugh about it but then on top of this Bob said he'd lost his wallet.

This was the second time in only a few days. Last time I'd found it under the mattress. We searched and searched but no luck and I went to bed feeling like chewed string. The next day we found it. He'd put it in a safe place between the books on his book shelves. As he had thousands of books, it was a miracle that we found it at all.

***

April was almost here. The world was coming out of winter. The lambs were springing in the fields but I had lost my spring. I was starting to plant and sow a few vegetables in the garden but my heart wasn't in it. I decided to go to Kira's for her birthday. I was desperate for a short break. Alexis, my younger daughter met me off the train and we drove to Kira's and had a little party together. While I was away the little car had to have its gearbox sent back to Lancashire – our garage people here were very nice but they didn't have the specialised knowledge to deal with such unusual cars.

Holger took me to the station. I hoped Bob would be alright but I was just glad to be away for a few days. To be honest I was feeling so low that I was past caring. At least, I thought, there won't be any mishaps with him driving the car while I'm away. I returned, refreshed, a few days later. The car had been mended and the weather was lovely. Bob was in a good mood and sang to me as we drove over to the beach at Trefor. It was a beautiful day.

We walked along the coast, looking at the gulls and cormorants. The lambs raced playfully towards us and then raced away. We sat near the edge of the cliff, drinking tea and munching apples and dates. It was like summer and the sea like a millpond. A little red fishing boat was bobbing gently in the bay. As we sat looking at the view Bob told me that he'd been to see the doctor while I was away. He told me that the doctor had suggested that he could bring me with him next time so on the way home from the beach we popped into the surgery and made an appointment.

A few days later we went to see Dr Jones. Later I wrote in my diary about this visit:

"While I was away Bob went to see the doctor on his own but he was upset and nervous so his ability to speak collapsed. Dr Jones suggested that I come with him next time. So I did.

Dr Jones looked at Bob's notes and showed me that the psychiatrist had written 'Frontal Lobe Dementia.' He said that this diagnosis could be confirmed if Bob had a scan. Bob was anxious to know if he could die from dementia. Dr Jones said that people don't die from dementia but I think that he was just being diplomatic. I have been reading up about frontal lobe dementia on the Internet. The frontal lobe controls the ability to speak, to think logically and to control one's moods. It looks as if it's a type of vascular dementia which comes about from the person suffering mini strokes which kill off brain cells. Possibly the scan would show up where Bob has had a mini stroke. It also says that as the brain gradually stops working, other parts of the body will be badly affected, so dementia does <u>indirectly</u> cause death. Bob also agreed to go back to the Memory Clinic and was put on a waiting list."

***

Getting some sort of diagnosis was strangely comforting. This beast now had a face. We would face it together Bob and I, come what may. Bob would not be alone. I would fight this with him.

A few days later I cycled down to Llyn Nantlle and walked along the side of the lake to the other end where the stream falls down from the mountain. I lay down by the waterside and let the sound wash through me. Memories of when Bob was well came flooding back to me. I remembered times back in Cornwall, how

Bob would service his motorbike on an old sheet in his flat, meticulously unscrewing nameless parts, carefully placing parts into various containers, his hands covered in black oil, and when it was all oiled and lubricated correctly he would put it all back together again. Now he struggled to even pump up his bicycle tyres and a few days ago when the chain came off his bike, he ended up pushing it all the way home because he couldn't remember how to put the chain back on.

I sat and sat, letting the memories wash through me. Then I wrote this poem.

Sound, Unsound

What is the opposite of sound?
Unsound?
Water ripples round the rocks
in my brain.
Words are hopeless.

A brook babbles.
Sheep bleat.
A quack ducks.
A quack ducks?

Frontal lobe dementia:

that's what he has

and   there is

not much

        we can   do

    but watch him slide

and slide

stumbling over words,

        laughing at jokes

only

        he understands.

He fumbles over zips.

Jumbles up his buttons,

frustration rumbling,

becoming volcanic anger.

But -

with a little tea or coffee washing it down,

languor takes him over.

I sit by the water,

sluice the ache,

feel

the movement,

a burbling of ripples,

mindlessly

washing the rocks.

May came and with it came warm sunshine. It was polling day and Bob and I went to vote. Bob was agitated and got in a muddle.

"I've forgotten my glasses," he explained to the man. He had put his cross in the wrong box. The man let him rub it out and try again. I wondered whether they would accept the voting slip. Did it really matter? What really mattered to me was that we were now sitting at the other end of the lake on a beautiful day and I was going to have my first swim of the year. It would probably be cold and my skin would tingle, but I would feel really alive. And Bob was happy now; he was munching an apple and listening to the birds singing. What was more important: a voting slip or this?

A few days later Bob went down with shingles on his chest and his back. We had to go to the Out of Hours Surgery at Bangor hospital as it was Bank Holiday Monday. He had complained that he had a rash on his chest. I didn't know what it was. Then it spread to his back and started to come up in little blisters. It was very painful and by then I guessed it was shingles as I'd had them myself. By this time it was one o'clock in the morning so as soon as it was daytime we drove to the hospital. Trust Bob to be ill like this on a bank holiday, poor love!

A few days after, Bob took the rest of the tablets for his shingles all at the same time. I worried that with so many tablets inside him he might get ill, but he didn't seem to be having any side effects from the overdose. The blisters were enormous and perhaps he'd thought, in his illogical way, that lots of tablets would make the pain go away. He was understandably very grumpy. A few days later I finally managed to persuade him to see our own doctor who gave him painkillers and E45 cream. He'd been in such pain and had spent a lot of time slumped in front of the television but the painkillers really helped and after a week or so he was up and about again. He caught the bus to Caernarfon and went around the charity shops and bought another book and a CD. The next afternoon was bright and sunny after all the rain so we went for a little walk up onto the hill above the Fairy Wood. Bluebells were everywhere and the bracken was just beginning to unfurl and I found my first foxglove peeping out of its small buds of pink and white. On the way home Bobby made me laugh. He said he'd stepped on a platitude!

On Malapropism

Could you call a cow pat a platitude?

I suppose you might, if it feels right.

It does have a certain attitude

of flatness, of not quite a pancake,

so maybe I should allow you some latitude,

and not put my foot in it with you.

In June we went off for a short holiday in our campervan, Charlie. I'd had to have some rather costly repairs done but at last Charlie was road worthy again and we set off for a spot not far from Aberdaron on the Llyn Peninsula. Bob was still a bit grumpy with pains from his shingles, poor man. We went to Whistling Sands and then drove to the far end of the peninsula where we had a wonderful view of Bardsey Island. The hillside was covered in foxgloves, hundreds of them. They were magnificent. We met some 'Born Again Christians' who were actually lapsed Catholics, like Bob. He told them about his shingles and they said they would pray for him. They were quite sweet people. One of them, Mary, said she was writing a book and calling it 'Life after Catholicism'.

The next day we went to Aberdaron church and I bought a book of R.S.Thomas's poems. He was the vicar there in the 1960s and '70s.

Aberdaron is a pleasant little place and after our visit to the church we walked along the coast and back. Then we bought fish and chips and drove the van to where we had a good view of the sunset. Bobby actually managed to make love to me for the first time in ages. I think we both enjoyed it. It was good to feel so close again. Our love making had nearly always been so wonderful but recently I had just been too tired and I think Bob had been so stressed by his shingles and the dementia that he hadn't felt like having sex either.

The following day he kept asking if we could go home. We'd had a lovely couple of days and I would have liked to stay longer but I thought he might get into a state. I could see he felt insecure, almost frightened. This was probably just another side of his dementia so we headed for home.

On the way the van started making funny noises. I stopped to see what it was and realised that the exhaust seemed to be hanging down a bit. Bob climbed underneath and bent it upwards and then we carried on. However, a mile or so further on, there was a big clatter and the exhaust fell off. We'd just passed a garage so I called in. The man at the garage said he only sold petrol but he also said it wouldn't matter driving without an exhaust for a bit but that I should get it fixed as soon as possible. Oh no, another bill to pay!

Then Alexis came to stay for a while. I had lots to do before she came. I wanted to have most of my chiropody work out the way and the house and garden tidy so that we could enjoy some time together. Bob wanted to help but really he was more of a hindrance. One time I asked him to wash the windows but instead he spent half the day scrubbing a wall. I asked him to water the polytunnel. Perhaps I should have said to please water *the inside* of the polytunnel. I found him watering all around the outside when it had only just stopped raining. Then he turned the stove off when I was in the middle of cooking a meal.

Alexis was with us for Bob's 70th birthday so we went to Sopna for his birthday dinner. Sopna had won an award for the best Welsh curry house and Bob and Alexis both loved a good curry.

Inevitably I had a tummy ache. I think I had eaten too much!

It rained most of Bob's birthday so we spent some of the day shopping. Alexis bought Bob a flowering plant ...Bob loved flowers... and I bought him a new sweater. There had been heavy rain all over the country with floods in some places, mainly in the midlands and northern England. It wasn't that bad in Wales.

A few days later we left Alexis doing some studying for her Art Degree course and went to see the specialist, Doctor Kurian at the hospital. I thought it would be a good idea to write down a list of questions that I wanted to ask him.

I sat out in the garden the morning before the hospital appointment, thinking about what to ask but somehow I didn't seem to be able to think of anything. Maybe the scan Bob had finally agreed to have would answer more questions but if it was vascular dementia, I knew from reading about it that there was very little that could be done. The information I'd found online talked about exercise, both physical and mental. I'd constantly encouraged Bob to keep reading and writing so he wouldn't forget how. We'd go out walking; he'd help me in the garden. Then it talked about a healthy diet. Generally he ate lots of healthy things ...though he did love pork pies and chips but he didn't eat them more than maybe once a week at most. I tried to encourage him to play chess which he used to be brilliant at, but I was useless at chess and he didn't want play with anyone else now. He'd get embarrassed by his mistakes. My head seemed to be all over the place. Was I going crazy too? In the end I just wrote this poem.

Dementia gardening

There are many types of dementia.
I must move those pebbles,
they'll damage the lawn mower.
Alzheimer's is the most common.
I don't think he has that.

Those brambles need pulling up
before they grow too big.
About three people in twenty with dementia
have vascular dementia.

The camellia's dropping petals,
pink petals going brown. It looks a mess.
Small strokes or blockages cause brain cells to die.
The pond's going green.

It can begin slowly and worsen over time.
Sometimes it comes on rapidly.
But the water mint is growing well.
Emotions may be changeable,
and can be unpredictable.

The sun's come out.

Those plants need watering.

Ten percent will have hallucinations.

I'd better go in. I think it's going to rain.

Ninety percent will have obsessions.

I'll check the tadpoles first.

There aren't so many now.

Sleep patterns are often abnormal.

Something must be eating them.

The night after the hospital appointment I sat up in bed, writing up some of the work for my M.A. I had been going to the course most Tuesday evenings and was really enjoying the mental stimulation even though my writing wasn't particularly good. Now, in the middle of the night I was finding it impossible to sleep and impossible to study. I kept pondering over the events of the previous day when Bob and I went to see Doctor Kurian. As I couldn't sleep I wrote up my diary:

"Bob did very badly in all the tests for his brain and Doctor Kurian said he may have Alzheimer's but it was much more likely to be vascular dementia. Bob also had an ECG and blood tests and we have to see Doctor Jones in two weeks and Doctor Kurian in two months. Bob reneged on the CT again but then later said that he ought to 'bite the bullet', so we went back after a cup of coffee in the hospital snack bar to tell Bethan in the Memory Clinic. She said that there was a waiting list so it won't happen that quickly anyway.

Doctor Kurian also asked about Bob's driving. I said it was okay-ish and also explained about his motorbike and him forgetting how to start it. He hasn't been out on it for ages. Doctor Kurian gave Bob a letter that says he is not to drive the motorbike anymore and that when it comes to the car he is only to drive locally, not at night, not in busy traffic and not alone. I found it difficult to tell Bob but he has agreed to sell the motorbike. I wonder if Dafydd might buy it. He was saying he needs a better bike."

A couple of days later Alexis and I drove down to Cornwall together in Charlie, the campervan. It meant we could share the driving and the cost of the fuel and it gave me a chance to see the rest of the family briefly before driving on my own back to Wales.

On the drive home I did wonder what new chaos might greet me with Bob's dementia getting worse but I had a nice surprise. No new chaos greeted me. Bob had cleaned the house, cooked a meal and mowed the lawn! Well most of the lawn was mowed. He couldn't remember how to fill the petrol tank so once it had run out of fuel he'd put the lawn mower away in the garage, but most of it was done.

When I looked at the calendar the next morning I realised it was July 10th. Five years ago we'd moved to Wales, full of happiness and high hopes. A whole five years had gone by and life was definitely not what I had hoped for.

The next night Bob had prepared another evening meal. I was so glad as I had had a busy day at work but this time it was a very strange meal. It was a combination of puréed beetroot and raspberries, with raspberries and strawberries on top covered with a garnish of chopped garlic! He seemed very pleased with his meal. I tried it but I just couldn't eat it. I pushed the garlic to one side while Bob ate his share with relish. I didn't want to hurt his feelings so I tried a little more but it tasted awful.

"Sorry, Bobby, I'm just not very hungry. You can eat mine if you like."
And he did!

Another day I went out for a walk and came back to find that Bob had gone off in the little car. He was not supposed to drive alone now. When he came back I found he'd gone all the way to Bangor to make an appointment at Specsavers when I'd already made an appointment for him. He was very upset with himself for forgetting, poor man. I was more concerned about him driving alone when the doctor had told him not to, but I didn't tell him that. Also his eyesight had got a lot worse. The opticians were going to give him bi-focals or vari-focals. I hoped they would work for him. He really needed to wear them all the time but he probably wouldn't.

***

Soon after this Kira and her boyfriend Brett broke up and she was very upset. My neighbours Andy and Deb were also upset because their dog Jazz was ill and then my old friend Dinah phoned and she sounded very upset and depressed too. I suggested that Bob and I visit her and she cheered up at that idea. She lived near Aberystwyth. . We could spend some time with her and then go on to Pembrokeshire. I had heard that the coast of Pembrokshire was beautiful and Bob seemed to like the idea of another trip in Charlie

The holiday started so well. It was lovely to see Dinah and her husband. The next day we went to a campsite near Cardigan and had a lovely walk on the coastal path. We then went on to St David's. The Bournemouth Symphony orchestra were practising in the cathedral so we stayed for the concert. It was truly wonderful: Elgar and Mendelson – beautiful music in a magical setting.

Then we went back to a campsite near Spittal and suddenly Bob became very moody and confused. He complained that there was blue stuff in the toilet and no hot water in the basin. I showed him how to use the shower, which was nice and hot but he just didn't seem to be able to cope with having a shower. It was as if he'd gone back in time to the days when he had to have a strip wash and showers didn't exist and he became very, very grumpy. I think we were both tired. Charlie was not the most convenient van. Bob was tall and the bed was not long enough so every night I would make a platform for his feet out of the cool box and a piece of sponge.

And we both had to get up in the night for a pee in the bucket but nowadays poor Bob always struggled like a beached whale, cursing slightly and sometimes not so slightly.

Next morning, we ended up having a row. I gave him the money to pay for our camping and he went off to pay Mr Marshall who owned the campsite. He came back saying he'd made a mistake and paid too much. But Mr Marshall came over very upset because we hadn't paid enough! It was all very difficult so I told him that Bob had made a mistake because he had dementia. He was then very understanding but Bob was mortified and furious with me.

"You shouldn't have told him I had dementia!"

"But Bobby, he was very understanding about things... about the mistake you made once he knew..."

"I don't want you telling people!"

"But sometimes it helps for people to know."

"I'm not having you telling everybody!"

"Okay, okay...I'm sorry..."

Bob was angry all the way home. And I felt so down and depressed. I went off and slept in the other room and cried myself to sleep. In the morning I wrote:

"If only these tears could wash away the problems in your brain my dear beloved one. If only I could let go of all myself that feels this pain. Drain myself of all my longing, for the 'what might have been'. Let go of hope and aspirations. Take up this moment. I have only this moment to hand."

Later I spoke to my grandchildren on the phone. Amber and Jasper also sounded so unhappy. I wished I could be there to help but the roads to Cornwall would be choked with holiday traffic and I just couldn't face the journey or leaving Bob yet again. It would Jasper's birthday very soon and I wouldn't be there.

After our return from Pembrokeshire, Bob's ability to speak seemed worse. He found it so difficult to tell me things and often I just didn't understand what he was trying to say. I knew it must be awful for him too but in my depressed state, it just made me cry and cry. It was very selfish of me but then depression is a selfish state...

Bob preparing vegetables for dinner

Chapter 6

Officialdom Begins

Bob and I had a long discussion one afternoon after which he agreed to sell his motorbike (which he was no longer allowed to drive). We also talked about selling the house and finding something smaller and more manageable. He seemed quite happy with these decisions so we advertised the motorbike in the local newspaper and put the house in the hands of an estate agent. Although I did still miss Cornwall, I didn't think we should move back there. It would probably make Bob's dementia worse. He was happy in North Wales and he definitely didn't want to move far so we had a look at some of the houses that were for sale nearby.

Every night I would go to bed unsure if I would be woken at some unearthly hour. Sometimes I would have a good night's sleep, but other nights I wouldn't. Around this time I wrote in my diary:

"It's 4:15 a.m. and I'm not sleeping. About an hour ago, I woke up to hear Bob running a basin full of water. I got up to see what he was doing.

"Bobby... it's not time to get up and have a wash. It's the middle of the night."

"Oh Christ!" He said angrily.

It felt as if he was angry at me or maybe he was just angry with himself, who knows. He so often gets angry nowadays. He stomped back to bed. I went downstairs to get a drink and when I went back to the bedroom he had pulled most of the covers onto his side. I tried to take some back over my side but he just grabbed them tightly and made angry noises.

"Bob, could I have some of the covers please?"

But there was no answer. Somehow, he was already asleep. I went off to the other bedroom muttering about what a nasty mean man he was. He never stirred even when I came back to get my book. This is not the real Bob.

This is the illness, so I must try not to take his behaviour personally but I hurt inside even in the midst of telling myself that his behaviour is nobody's fault."

Every day would bring new challenges for me and Bob. I was never sure what he would do next so I would encourage him to come with me when I went out to work, but he didn't always want to come and there was no way I could make a stubborn, strong, big man do something he didn't want to do so I would try to suggest fun things for him to do if he did come with me. One day we took a pile of bread that our neighbours Andy and Deb had given us... far too much for Quack to eat... and after I'd finished work we went down to the quay. There were a few seagulls and a couple of swans but very soon there were about thirty swans, lots of ducks and pigeons and seagulls all eager for our bread. It was an amazing sight. So many swans all swimming towards us.

Bob loved it. He was just like a big kid throwing the bread baps like frisbees up into the air and shouting, "Whey hey!" It was only afterwards when we walked further down towards the castle that I saw the sign: "Please don't feed the birds." Ooops, I thought. I didn't tell Bob!

But inevitably there were many days that I went out to work on my own.

One day I left about 8:30 – Bob was still in bed when I left – and I didn't get back until the afternoon. On return I found that Bob had gone and so had his motorbike! Oh shit, I thought, he's gone out on it! And he's not supposed to ride it anymore. I wasn't sure what to do. I asked some of the neighbours but no one had seen him go. I told myself, "He'll be back soon. He'll be fine". I threw myself into doing things to keep from worrying. I weeded the garden for a bit and then picked some runner beans and dug up some potatoes. I fed the hens and Quack and Heidi. I did some cleaning and prepared food for our evening meal. It was getting late. I jumped at every sound of a vehicle. It was evening and the sun was starting to set and he was still not home. I tried to think "Well, no news is good news... it's a lovely day and although he's not supposed to ride the motorbike anymore, I'm sure he's fine. Perhaps, somewhere he's watching the sunset like me". But another part of me was trying not to think; "He might be dead."

For a moment I had an awful thought: life would be a lot simpler if he was dead, both for him and for me. He wouldn't have to suffer the frightening and confusing thing that was happening to him and I wouldn't have to watch the man I loved so much changing and dissolving into some other form of himself that I no longer felt I knew. But then I immediately felt a great hole in my heart at such an awful thought. If he was no more, this man I loved so much, despite all the difficulties... how much I would miss him and then I found myself praying fervently that he would be okay.

Then I rang the police. They were very understanding and efficient but they had no reports of an accident. However, they did take down his details. I told them about his dementia and how he was not supposed to be using the motorbike anymore. "But he probably forgot." They said they would look out for him but I didn't really believe them. I thought to myself. "There are very few police in this part of Wales and they're probably all too busy dealing with serious criminals and filling in forms." Well anyway, Bob would now be down on their files as a 'vulnerable adult.' They told me to phone them back as soon as he came home.

I went out into the lane and watched the sun sink like a lozenge melting into the sea. What would tomorrow bring? Would he be home by then? I spoke to my neighbours again. They were full of sympathy but they knew no more than me. The sun had gone. I heard an owl in the trees below my house. Sheep were bleating but where was my Bobby? I was sick with anxiety. I could not rest. I could not eat. I wanted to walk out but I needed to be near the phone in case the police phoned me or Bob returned. And then, oh what a relief! In the dark I saw Deb's car draw up outside her house and out stepped Bobby! I flew into his arms and hugged him tight. My dear neighbour and friend, Deb, had found him walking home from Caernarfon. He'd walked as far as Inigo Jones and it was just getting dark.

"It was lucky I saw him," said Deb. "He's left the bike at the garage by Tesco's. He says it won't start."

The next day we picked it up from the garage. There was nothing wrong with it. He'd just forgotten how to start it, yet again.

***

A few days later, Ariel rang to ask if he and his new girlfriend could come to stay and bring Amber and Jasper with them. He was still into the raw food diet and I had to promise not to feed the children on cooked food otherwise he wouldn't come. I did wonder how on earth I was going to explain to Bob that he must not give the children any cooked food but I was sure we'd manage. It was almost the end of August when they came. The weather was dry and sunny so we all went to the beach. I was so happy to see my grandchildren again but they were not at all happy with their father insisting they only ate raw food. I decided that the best thing was for Bob and I to eat our cooked food in Bob's little kitchen so we wouldn't be eating cooked food in front of them. Then we would eat some nice salads with them some of the time.

About three days into their stay we woke up to find that the girlfriend had left. Ariel said that she found the children difficult. Well, I thought to myself, they are missing their mother and missing cooked food and so yes, they are being difficult. Ariel said that his girlfriend had all sorts of problems and that maybe it was all for the best as she didn't really like children but he was still very upset that she'd gone. Anyway, Bob and I took the children to Caernarfon Castle so Ariel could sort himself out and make sure the girlfriend was okay. We had a lovely time, though Amber did manage to get lost for a bit and Bob became extremely anxious. He loved Amber, like she was really his own granddaughter. He wanted to rush around the castle but there were so many passages. I said that it would be best to tell the people in charge that she had gone missing and wait by the entrance. I had great difficulty persuading him just to be patient and stay put. Every minute he was ready to rush off. Jasper was as good as gold and stayed by my side. Bob was more difficult to reason with.

"Bobby, if you go off looking for her then we will lose you too. There are so many different ways to go. She will come back to the entrance very soon, I'm sure." After about ten minutes, minutes that seemed like hours with Bob straining at the leash, Amber appeared, looking worried and relieved to see us. We decided to leave the castle then and went to find the little shop that sold homemade ice cream. Then the children had a ride on the lovely old carousel in the Maes and I took some photos of them going round and round.

A few days later Bob and I went for a walk up Mynedd Craig Goch. The family had gone home and though it had been lovely to see them, it was peaceful now they'd gone. I went ahead of Bob and sat on a rock at the top to wait for him. I got my diary out and started to write. I watched the clouds, fair weather clouds, gently moving across the sky making patterns and shapes. One looked like a little dog and the other a bit like a dragon chasing after it. Bob was nearer now. I was glad he was taking his time. I thought to myself, "I've noticed recently that he doesn't have the sense of balance that he used to have. He fell over several times when we were coming down Y Garn the other day and cut his knee and his hand so it's best he takes his time. I don't want him to fall again today. I worry, wondering how much longer he will be able to get out onto the mountains like this. He loves to be up here so much. I wonder if he thinks about it or if he is just enjoying the moment. I should be enjoying this moment too, the sun shining, the beautiful view, and not worrying about the future."

I got out the flask and two mugs when he eventually arrived. "Tea, Bobby?"

He smiled, "Yes please." I started to pour. "You've got the sandwiches."

"Oh yes." He took his sack off and opened the top. He fished around inside for the two chunky sandwiches and handed one to me. I handed him his tea and we sat quietly munching and supping our tea.

"I've been watching the clouds. There's one over there that looked

113

like a dog and the one behind was a dragon but they've changed shape again. I think they've turned into ordinary clouds now."

Bob looked at the clouds. "Maybe the one at the back looks a bit like a... ...like a bear...?"

He started to hum and after a little while he stood up and burst into song. I felt he was singing to the whole world or a least to the mountain.

I clapped my hands. "That's beautiful, Bobby," I said when he'd finished. "Isn't that one of the arias we heard at the Faenol festival the other day?"

"Yes," he smiled.

We'd been to the festival with Gillian and Holger again this year and Bob had said it was the best ever as there was a wonderful line-up of singers. He'd clapped and shouted 'bravo' as he always did and I'd just felt happy to see him so happy. And now here he was, happy again, singing on the top of a mountain.

A few days later I fell asleep during the last night of the proms. Bob and I always enjoyed watching it together and it seemed especially important now, with his dementia, as it was in music that we could share most. It didn't require reading or speaking. So I was annoyed with myself for falling asleep.

Later, when I got into bed, I couldn't get to sleep so I moved into the spare bedroom to read my book... I loved to escape into a good book whenever I could... and then I decided to do some writing. The next module of my M.A. course would be starting soon and I needed to jot down a few ideas. It was going well. Tuesday evenings were something to look forward to and I couldn't wait for the term to start again. I wrote:

"It's almost midnight... no it's gone midnight. In these small wee hours, I am sitting here wondering what life is all about. I do believe in a creator but the one thing I feel really, really sure about is that loving kindness is what makes the world go round and to keep being loving often requires a lot of letting go of any expectations, any judgements. Accepting our failings and trying to live our own truth and yet accepting that others have their way, their truth, which may seem wrong to us, but not judging them, for who are

we to judge? We cannot see the bigger picture. In terms of infinity and eternity what are we? We are just tiny dots living on a bigger dot."

Full Stop

I have come to a full stop.

I am

a small dot......

I am so small you cannot see me

out there

in the universe.

I hardly exist.

You hardly exist,

and yet I matter to me.

You matter to you.

We are each the centre

of our own universe,

smaller and smaller,

inside each of us,

amazingly made.

Made of dots,

lots,

my dots and your dots.

Dotty dot dot dot.

Full stops, dotty dot. dot. dot. dot. dot. dot. dot dot dot dot.........

I read this diary entry to Bob and he said it was good. He seemed more normal and more like his old self the next day. It was a good day. I found myself looking back to a time when we could have had deep discussions about the meaning of life. We would read and share our thoughts on the psychological ideas of Jung and Freud and the philosophy of people like Viktor Frankl, Joseph Campbell, Deepak Chopra and others. We read books together on Sufism, Buddhism, Hinduism and also books by mystical Christian writers such as Julian of Norwich. Although Bob generally shunned organised religion after the strictures of his Catholic upbringing, he always searched after meaning and found it in poetry, in books on mystical thought but most of all in music and song. He never had my deep certainty of a creator and of life after life, but he had a much more grounded side to him than me and sometimes would say. "Come down off cloud nine, Ali!" However he always had an open mind and I so, so missed the deep conversations we used to have.

Bob was still able to read a bit and was trying hard to read a book about how to make money. He had become a bit obsessed about money and liked to go to his bank in Caernarfon to get printouts of his bank statement. He would then stare at the statement and ask the cashier to explain what it all meant. He liked to take money out and then would sometimes go back the same day or the next day and put it back in. He liked to do all this over the counter and when I went into the bank with him, I was amazed at how patient the people were with him. He, despite his memory loss, was always so polite and friendly and everyone seemed to be fond of him. I was deeply grateful for their patience.

The house was on the market now, but so far we had not had anyone come to look at it. A smaller house and garden would make things easier. We cycled around and looked at a few houses in Talysarn and Nantlle just to get some ideas. The other thing I decided to do was to see the solicitor to sort out Enduring Power of Attorney (It is now called Lasting Power of Attorney). The law was about to change making power of attorney harder to obtain and as Bob was finding it harder and harder to do things like write a cheque, the sooner it was sorted the better.

The solicitor was wonderfully patient with Bob and his struggle to find words. I had spoken to the solicitor on the phone to explain the situation and he had told me that the power of attorney needed to be sorted out while Bob still had the mental capacity to agree to it himself. Then, when he no longer had the mental capacity to deal with his financial affairs, I would be able to look after his finances for him. In order for Bob to feel happy to sign, I suggested to the solicitor that we also take out a power of attorney for me so that Bob could officially look after my affairs if I became mentally incapacitated. The solicitor raised his eyebrows a bit. "Are you quite sure?" he asked. But I knew that it was the only way we could get through this without Bob feeling that his pride was being dented, so I fixed a steely look on the solicitor. "Yes." I said and so it was all signed and sealed. The only other thing I had to do was to write a letter to the Office of the Public Guardian to explain why I was taking charge of Bob's affairs and not one of his relations. This was what I wrote:

Dear Sir/Madame,

I am Mr Robert Treves' friend and carer. I have known Robert for approximately 18 years. He is now 71 years old. He had moved to the village where I lived namely St Erth, in Cornwall and was unemployed and quite depressed at the time. As I was working for our local church as a "befriender" I got to know him well and he has been a close friend ever since.

He had a very tragic childhood. His mother had married again after the death of his father at Dunkirk. His mother was in a reserved occupation in London and he and his sister called Betty were sent to Catholic homes in the countryside. After the birth of his stepbrother David the family moved to Birmingham. The stepfather took to drink and was regularly violent, especially towards his mother. Robert was placed in another Catholic home,

Father Hudson's, now notorious for the abuse that took place there, and later he was sent to Borstal for stealing a bike on which to escape from another outbreak of violence at home. The Borstal recognized a clever boy and he was able to take day release and studied for his 'O' and 'A' levels and then went to London University. However at the age of about 20, his mother died and he left.

*For the next 30 years or so, before I met him in Cornwall, he travelled around Britain, picking up a job here and there and walking the mountains when he wasn't employed, with his house on his back, intent on being free from any of the normal trappings of society. He was also an angry man and his way of dealing with relationships was to walk away when anything upset him. When his sister married and moved house without telling him, he took it very personally and decided that he never wanted to see her again. His stepbrother David tried to make peace between them, but then he decided to break off contact with David as well. By now he was about 23 to 24 years old. He cannot remember his sister's married name or David's surname. He has blotted out so much of his past. Robert is now 71 years old and therefore has had no contact whatsoever with his sister and stepbrother for over 47 years. When I first knew him I suggested several times that he should try to regain contact with Betty and David, but he said **he never** wanted to see them again. Now that he has dementia he is not able to throw more light on the subject. Also, because he has tramped about the land he has no photos or records from that time.*

It would therefore be impossible to track down his sister and stepbrother.

Yours sincerely

***

A week later I decided go on a yoga and meditation weekend as I was badly in need of a break. I wrote in my diary.:

"Bob got up very early again today and I found him at 6:40 wearing three shirts, one on top of another! I did manage to gently persuade him to take them all off and put his vest and one shirt on. He's now decided to vacuum and is very busy vacuuming around the sofa so I'm being joggled a bit. He's been wonderful apart from the shirts. He cut up all the runner beans I picked so I can freeze them down. Then he swept the kitchen and now he's vacuuming with great gusto... my dear kind man. Yesterday he kept locking the door that he was trying to go through. Then I told him I was going to the farm shop in Penygroes to get a gate hinge. Would he be very kind and bring the washing in? On the way home, I met him furiously peddling his bike to Penygroes.

"Where are you going?"

"You said I was to go to the farm shop to get... Something."

I don't think he even knew what I had been going to buy. He'd probably have had the whole shop in uproar looking for something I didn't want, dear man. Thank goodness I met him! He turned his bike around and furiously peddled back home after my car. He then helped me with the hinge. I held it in place while he screwed.

"You like screwing," I said and we both giggled.

***

The weekend away did me good. Meditating in a group is always more powerful and I felt very relaxed and Bob had managed quite well on his own with our friends and neighbours keeping an eye on him. He was still studying his book on money when I got back and said I should read it! I said I would, just to please him. Later I found him enjoying watching children's cartoons on the TV. He'd always had a side to him that was quite childlike and he loved reading children's stories to the grandchildren but these cartoons? Maybe they were more than enough for his brain to cope with. I didn't know what else to do so I sat and watched with him but then I realised he'd fallen asleep so I went in the kitchen and upstairs and around the garden to check that everything was okay.

Bob had remembered to feed the 'creatures.' Upstairs looked all okay but when I checked the fridge he hadn't eaten very much so I decided to make a casserole with all the food that needed eating up. While I was cutting up vegetables, Kira phoned to ask me if I'd received her birthday parcel. She said she was sorry it was late but it should have arrived while I was away. She giggled when I said. "It might be in the dustbin." And it was. (We had a big black dustbin outside the front door that was not for rubbish but for parcels that were too big to go through the letterbox. People often thought it was funny but it was very useful).

I had fun opening it with her on the other end of the phone. There were some packets of lovely herbal tea, some Cornish ginger biscuits and a bubble blowing pot! She said "I think Bob might enjoy the bubbles".

The next day was difficult. Bob couldn't remember how to work the CD player. I tried to show him but he shouted at me and then swore at me. He had been having more and worse mood swings. Sometimes he was like a happy child and other times like a child having a temper tantrum.

Later on, we went for a walk along the beach at Aberdesach. I thought it would cheer him up but then he got into a tizz about his purse. He said he'd lost it. It wasn't in his pocket. He only noticed because he said he'd like to buy us both a cup of tea at the little mobile café. I searched everywhere in the car, but it wasn't there so we went home. I found it under a box of tissues on the table.

***

My friend Frieda, who had been looking after her mentally and physically disabled partner, Ray, for several years, was a bit of an expert on how to get help as she had worked both as a carer and for Social Services in the course of her life. She told me to phone the Memory Clinic and ask for help. She said that I should be eligible for some help, but that I needed to ask. She said "You have to keep asking for help otherwise you won't get it, and it's important to give them the worst-case scenario". So I phoned them and they said that they are going to get onto Social Services. I did hope there might be some help out there, but Bob's behaviour was probably not bad enough just yet.

Then a letter arrived for Bob from the DVLA saying that from the 20th October he was not allowed to drive anymore. It seemed strange to think that my dear man would not drive ever again. Bob had also agreed to sell his motorbike to Dafydd. He said he would take the bike down to him in the morning. Dafydd was paying him £150. It was worth more but Bob and I were very happy about it going to Dafydd. We were both very fond of him.

Bob also had the appointment for his CT scan in a week or so... at long last.

In November Kira came to stay with her new boyfriend Angel. He was a tall man and seemed to be good for her. Rosy and Amber came too but not Jasper. They were only staying for a couple of days but Angel was very kind and mended my fridge.

Then it was Remembrance Sunday and we watched a TV programme about war and Wilfred Owen, the 1st World War poet. I find his poetry very moving. After the programme we talked about the two world wars and then Bob suddenly told me an extraordinary thing. He had been sitting in his comfy chair earlier in the day and was suddenly aware, quite strongly, that his father, his real father, who was killed at Dunkirk when Bob was four, was standing beside him. He called him, "my old man". He said that his old man said to him, "I'm watching over you, my boy".

Bob had no memory of his father except for a few photos and letters that his mother shared with him when he was a child. One photo stayed in his memory... long since lost... it was of his father holding the baby Bob aloft, and they were both chortling at each other, a brief moment of joy. Whether he really saw his 'old man' or not, this experience gave Bob a lot of comfort and lifted his spirits for a while.

I wrote in my diary that evening:

"Here my Bob fights his own battle with his memory. When he reads now... and he keeps on trying... it is like a young boy learning to read, stumbling over the words. I think I am accepting more, but every now and then, especially if someone gives me too much sympathy, I find myself fighting back the tears. Sometimes, when I am on my own , I have a really good cry. Sometimes I rage. Here is a really good man trying to keep his spirits up, a brave man, battling against a condition that has no cure, no end but down. Maybe in years to come there will be wonderful things that can be done but here and now I feel so helpless watching his brain dying slowly."

***

I walked the Nantlle ridge with my friend Eric the next day. It had rained and the rocks were slippery and I was chatting and wasn't concentrating. Suddenly I slipped and made a grab at the rocks.

I felt my shoulder muscles screaming but I hung on and Eric pulled me to safety. It was a scary moment as I could have fallen a long, long way. I rubbed arnica on my shoulder and carried on walking, but my shoulder was now very sore. I needed to rest it, but I had some work the next day so Bob was my 'muscles' and carried all my heavy chiropody equipment in and out of my patients' houses. He often came with me nowadays anyway as I didn't like leaving him too long. I was glad that social services were finally coming to see him. I hoped that they would offer some help. I hoped too, it would be the sort of help I needed – or Bob needed. I'd been worrying so much I'd given myself an upset stomach but Bob held my tummy and my sore shoulder with his lovely warm healing hands and I felt so comforted. He really had such healing in his hands, bless him.

Unfortunately he was restless again that night. I just wished he would sleep and not wake me up half the night. In the end I moved into the other room. I was finding it difficult to sleep comfortably anyway with such a sore shoulder. It had just gone 4 a.m. At 3:30 I found Bob up and dressed and the bed made. He was upset with himself when I told him what time it was. I lay in bed unable to go back to sleep. I found myself worrying again. I wanted to go to Cornwall just after Christmas with Bob, but would my family want him to stay? John, my ex, has said he would like to do something to help and staying with him and his wife Avis for a couple of days would be a great help, but would they mind Bob's odd behaviour. Kira had said we could stay but would she and Angel mind? Ariel's parents also said we could stay. Maybe it would be okay. I was also worried about the fact that my friend Helen and I had booked that trip to China. I thought, "Perhaps I shouldn't go. Bob wasn't too bad when we booked it, but I'm going to have to have help now, if I leave him for over two and a half weeks. He is definitely worse these last few weeks".

***

On November 20th Bob was assessed! We had a meeting with social services and Bob now had his own social worker called Angharad. She seemed nice and said I could call her anytime. They only offered me 4 hours a week of help so far and said that a carer would come to make Bob a meal by heating up a ready meal and that they could do some cleaning or washing up while they were at the house. I got in touch with the ready meal people and they said they would also provide a microwave as I didn't have one.

Around this time I conducted a rather silly experiment. I felt a bit ashamed of myself afterwards as I would never really cheat on Bob but I wanted to prove that Bob didn't forget like someone with Alzheimer's would. As he was always fussing and obsessing over money, I chose to take £20 out of his purse and hide it. The next day he opened his purse to find it gone.

"Where's my £20 note gone?"

I did a big pretence of searching for it until I 'found' it. I felt guilty for doing this but it did help me to feel fairly certain that his short-term memory was not totally impaired.

At the end of November we went to see Dr Kurian at the hospital to discuss the results of the CT scan. In some ways it all felt a waste of time. The results from the CT scan showed that he had had a slight stroke in his frontal lobe a few years ago. I told Dr Kurian that I had suspected as much but that it happened when we were moving house and nothing was done about it at the time. All that happened was that Bob had a bad headache after which he had mild dysphasia. I said to Dr Kurian twice that this did not really explain Bob's steady decline. He did not seem keen to explain why that should be. I had the impression that he found Bob's type of dementia complicated so perhaps he didn't know. Perhaps, I thought this poor doctor is fumbling in the dark almost as much as we are.

Perhaps I have to accept that despite the wonderful advances made in medical science, understanding of the brain is still in its infancy. Eventually he said that Bob could see the neurologist but that there was a waiting list of several months. I think we both left the hospital feeling frustrated and upset. Bob was difficult when we got home, fussing over the keys again: he started locking and unlocking doors. It had become another of his obsessions. I went upstairs and just sobbed and sobbed. I suppose I was hoping for some sort of certainty from Dr Kurian and from the results of the CT scan, but there was none. In the end I phoned one of my old friends in Cornwall for a chat. It was comforting to talk to her.

Bob had a series of bad nights after this and so I had difficulty sleeping too. I wrote:

"Bob woke me up an hour or so ago, worried that I was not yet up. He was washed and dressed; he'd made the bed and opened the curtains. Poor man, he took a bit of persuading that it was not the right time to get up, even though it was dark outside. I gave him a little reflexology which helped him go back to sleep. I think I will make a mug of valerian tea... maybe then I will sleep."

The next few nights were almost as bad. I had noticed over the last few months that Bob seemed to be having to get up to pee more and more frequently so maybe this was part of the problem. Sometimes he'd get up to pee three times in the night, maybe more. I told our GP about this last time we visited the surgery and he arranged an appointment for Bob to go to the Urology Department in January for it to be checked.

On top of everything else Bob would not agree to signing a cheque to pay for the ready meals. He said he didn't want to. He said he didn't want them. I ended up getting angry, trying to explain to him that the carers don't have time to cook him a proper meal and that I still needed to go out to work several days a week and I wanted them to come and help.

"I don't need their help!"

"Please Bobby."

Eventually he did sign three cheques so I wouldn't have to ask him again for a while. He was finding it harder to write and I knew there would come a time when he wouldn't be able to sign his name. By then I would probably be able to take over his financial affairs officially but in the meantime maybe I could ask him to give me his card number so I can draw out money from the hole in the wall. I hoped that we might go to Cornwall after Christmas but I would need him to share the cost of the trip and then there would be presents from us both for the children. I wrote in my diary:

"I can't work much now that he is as he is, and he has a lot of money in his bank account. I can't get carer's allowance because I'm receiving an old age pension and he is becoming very mean with money now. He owes me money, but he's convinced he's poor. I'm not prepared to pay for everything and I would never cheat him out of anything he doesn't owe me. He tried to make love to me tonight but it wasn't a great success. I was too tired. I feel upset. He is so unhappy about what is happening to him. I can't sleep as my IBS has flared up."

***

One thing that was making life more and more difficult at this time was the fact that I sometimes could not understand what Bob was saying. His words were so tangled and often they just made no sense to me at all. Often he would become very cross because I couldn't understand him. One day, for example he was trying to tell me that the leather fob on his key ring was broken but his words were so tangled up. I tried to guess but I got it wrong several times. "No, no no!" Eventually I did understand because he waved the keys in the air and pointed to the broken fob.

"Oh, you mean the fob, it's broken,"

"Yes," he said, exasperation written all over him.

"I'm sorry, I didn't understand you."

It was so frustrating for him. Well it was frustrating for us both.

Sometimes I would just pretend I understood what he was saying but that didn't always work either. I would ask him a question and he'd look surprised. "I've just told you that!"

Christmas was almost upon us so we went Christmas shopping. We bought each other Christmas presents and some things for the children which we planned to take with us to Cornwall. I did wonder about the wisdom of going to Cornwall. Looking back I can't think why we went. It was a really stupid thing to do with Bob's dementia getting worse and the weather was foul with rain and floods and I had a chesty cold. We stayed with John and Ariel's parents. But Kira and Angel didn't want us to stay and so we hardly saw the grandchildren and that made me feel very sad. Kira was not in a happy state of mind, still too unbalanced herself to cope with Bob staying at her house with his dementia, but we saw Alexis, my daughter, who was busy studying Art at Falmouth, and some of our old friends. I had wanted this trip to be a time to treasure, knowing in my heart that soon Bob would probably be too unwell and too difficult with his dementia to ever return again to Cornwall, but he was already too unwell to really appreciate the trip and I think it would have been better to have stayed in Wales.

Chapter 7

Descent

It was January 8th and we were at the hospital for Bob's appointment in the urology department. Bob was having a check-up for his prostate because he'd been peeing so frequently and he wouldn't bloody cooperate. All he had to do was to pee into a bottle for goodness sake! I held his hand and said, "Please Bobby". But I received one of his stony stubborn stares that would often be a precursor to another of his black moods. I gave up and stared at my feet and took some deep breaths. I knew he hated hospitals and any medical interference but it was not much to ask to just pee in a bottle. Anyway, the nurse was very good with him. She smiled and changed the subject and chatted away to him about the weather and things like that and then she took his blood pressure and asked various questions about how often he had to get up in the night to pee etc. Suddenly he was saying he needed a pee, so the nurse said.

"Well you can go in here then." Before he knew it, he had peed into their machine and done the test that they'd wanted him to do without him realising it. We then talked to the doctor who said he might have prostate cancer. They wanted him to come back the following Tuesday for an endoscopy. Oh heavens, I thought, what if he has a serious cancer on top of everything else? I tried not to worry but of course I did.

When I was in Cornwall, my friend Georgina lent me a book called 'The Secret' by Rhonda Bryne. I'm not sure what I thought of the book; it was no work of literature but the suggestions of giving oneself 'positive affirmations' seemed to help my state of mind a little but I still felt pretty depressed and frequently cried when I was on my own. I sent positive affirmations in my heart to all my family with their various problems and more especially to my Bobby. I pictured him being well and happy. Also I wanted a buyer for the house, so I also did some positive affirmations about that as well.

I was making a habit of getting up early even if I'd not had a good night's sleep. Bob was rarely up early so I would try to have time to meditate and work on finishing off bits of coursework for my M.A. I was planning on writing a long poem for my next big assignment. Writing helped me and I wrote this short poem one early morning when I was feeling very down:

The Floor Feels Nothing

When you cry, you cry
into the floor, which is hollow
and does not hear.
Did you know, when you fell,
is it called 'in love'
down onto it,
how much pain
you would feel – loving this man?

The floor feels nothing.

A few days later we went to the village pantomime. It was a wonderful light relief! They did 'Snow White and the Seven Dwarfs'. It was a big improvement on the previous year's panto and was great fun. Afterwards we went back to Gillian's and had a nice meal with them but I was very tired. The weather was foul and Bob was tiring, bless him. The day before he had hidden his wallet amongst his books again but we found it fortunately. I was getting so used to him hiding things amongst his books and though he had hundreds of them, he tended to choose similar places.

A few days later a lady came from the social services finance department about his money situation. She said he would get some sort of thing called 'attendance allowance'. I felt a bit out of my depth but any money was welcome now that I couldn't work very much.

Then there was the endoscopy. I was praying that Bob would be relaxed and cooperative about the whole thing. I did some more positive affirmations and afterwards I wrote in my diary:

"Bob had the endoscopy at the hospital. He was fine until they took him off on his own into the operating room. It's always a bit difficult when I tell them I'm not related to him. I can't officially say I'm his next of kin. I'm just his very close friend. So I wasn't allowed to go with him. It was an Indian doctor doing the endoscopy and he had a very strong accent. Bob may have found his speech difficult to understand. Anyway, in the end they called me in because he was refusing to cooperate.

The doctor told me that Bob had to sign a statement saying that they could do the procedure. So I tried to explain to Bob how it was important that he allowed them to check for cancer and that people die from prostate cancer but that it could be treated if he had it. But I could not frighten Bob into signing, so I then said: "Please Bobby, do it for me, otherwise I shall worry about it." And then he did a rather wobbly signature and they allowed me to stay with him from then on. All the nurses were very kind.

Afterwards, a nurse called Judith gave Bob some antibiotics to take. "Bob won't take them" I told her. "He doesn't believe in taking any tablets, nor do I if I can avoid them." She suggested he have lots of raw garlic instead as it's a natural antibiotic. She said she thought it was better anyway, good on her! I shall put lots of raw garlic on our food the next few days. On the way home, Bob said, "I'm glad I've had it done".

Bob with Quack in happier times

A few days later a very sad thing happened.

Quack was attacked by the little terrier dog that belonged to one of our neighbours. I heard a bit of a commotion in the garden and went to see what it was. It was a dull drizzly afternoon and the light was fading. I didn't see Quack at first but I saw the little dog with blood on its mouth. It ran away when it saw me. Then out of the gloom I heard a faint "Quack, quack." It was so faint. Then I saw her bloodied body and gathered her up into my arms and carried her into the house. Bobby just stared in dismay at what had happened to her. I wrapped her in a towel and then held her out to him. He looked at me blankly. Perhaps he didn't understand that I needed his help so I said, "Bobby, please will you hold her my love. You have such healing hands. It may help, my love." And then I added, "it was the horrid little dog next door attacked her. I need to check on the hens. I think it may have got them as well."

I ran all the way up the garden to find five very bedraggled hens. One was bleeding from its wing, another from its tail end and one had a bite on its neck. I rushed back and got some ointment and plastered their wounds and then shut them up for the night. None of their wounds looked too serious. Then I ran back to Bobby who was still sitting in the kitchen holding Quack. He looked at me and his face said it all. He had difficulty enough finding words nowadays but now he had no words at all. I gently took Quack from him. I held her in one arm and tried to sponge her wounds clean with some warm water but she had been bitten in so many places. I stroked her head and felt her go. Her head flopped sideways.

"Oh Quack," I sobbed. "My dear old duck." Bobby just sat and starred in stony silence. I wondered what was going through his mind. Maybe he was thinking back to his favourite 'creature' in childhood: a little cat called Tibbles which had been killed by some local louts or maybe he was just simply upset about Quack and couldn't find any words to say so.

Later I went to see my neighbour. He was very apologetic and offered to buy me another duck. He had no idea how I felt about

Quack. To him she was just any old duck but I couldn't help feeling very angry. They kept that dog chained up all the time, which probably made it more ferocious and very difficult to control when it broke free. Somehow it had got through the hedge and attacked the hens and Quack but I felt that they shouldn't keep a dog if they were going to have it chained up like that.

Memories of Quack came flooding back: Quack's delight when she first got a proper pond. At first she eyed it suspiciously, waddled around it. I don't think she'd ever had a pond, only a baby bath. She ducked her head at it, dipped her beak into it and then dived in with a loud approving quack. Bob and I chuckled as we watched her. Another time we were sitting on the grass having a picnic with Amber and Jasper. Amber was waving her remaining bit of sandwich as she talked; unaware that Quack had snuck up behind her. The naughty duck grabbed it out of her hand, gobbling it quickly as she ran off. Poor Amber was not happy at all but it was funny.

As Quack got older, being a heavy Aylesbury duck her legs began to buckle a bit under her weight. One day one leg refused to work at all and she came out of her hutch and promptly fell over. I picked her up and gently rubbed her leg. She didn't seem to mind and I couldn't see anything wrong so I put her down and she promptly fell over again. I went running in to Bob.

"Bobby, there's something wrong with Quack's leg. She can't walk."

Tears were starting in my eyes.

"Well, we must take her to the vet."

Quack was quite unfazed by the car journey. I drove and she sat on a towel on Bob's lap, just in case she pooped on him. She moved her head from side to side as we went, looking at everything. At the vet's she sat politely on Bob's lap, quacking gently and looking with interest at all the dogs and cats. I'm sure she thought she was one of them. Everyone in the waiting room wanted to make a fuss of her but she soon had had enough and pushed them away with a little jab of her beak. The vet thought she had sprained her leg and put her on the scales to see what quantity of medication she should have. Quack sat, tried to stand and then tipped over again.

"She's a little overweight too." He said.

So she had to go on a diet, poor Quack, but she recovered well. She must've been 15 at least when she died. She was pretty old when we adopted her.

To Quack

I shall miss you Quack, my dear old duck,

ducking your head at my window for food.

You loved our attention, imperious one,

But give you too much and you'd spurn it.

With a wag of your tail you'd waddle away.

I shall miss your loud "quack quack" at

the sound of the gate, just like a dog

you'd come to your name, waggling your tail,

looking quizzically at us with your beady eye.

You'd soften the hardest of hearts without fail.

Enjoy quack heaven, for I know you should

 be guzzling the juiciest worms with your beak,

ducking and diving in mud, like any duck would.

We now had another grave at the top of the garden. Bobby dug the hole and I gently placed Quack into it. I had wrapped her body in a cloth and placed her in a large box.

"Goodbye Quack." I said as Bob shovelled soil and rocks on top of her. We later planted some daffodils on top of her grave.

"Well," I said to Bobby as we walked back down the garden hand in hand, "Life, as they say, must go on."

Whenever Andy and Deb were away we looked after their dog, Jazz. She was a lovely natured springer spaniel and we were both very fond of her. Also when Andy and Deb were out all day Bob and I would often enjoy taking her out on walks up to the quarry and across the fields. After Quack died, her happy fun loving waggling tail cheered us up whenever we took her out with us. Sometimes we'd take her in the car a little way up the road to the Beddgelert forest and then we would walk up to the lake. There were no sheep there so she could run free and usually got extremely muddy. Whenever we'd had a good walk, either with or without Jazz, I would hope that Bob would sleep well but usually it seemed to make little difference. He would regularly wake up at 2 a.m. and then 4 a.m. but if I was lucky he might sleep till 5 or 6 a.m. Each time he woke he would start to get washed and dressed and would be very grumpy with me when I told him that it was far too early to get up.

Once, after a few days of us looking after Jazz while they were away, Andy and Deb came home and told us they were thinking of selling the house they let, which was next door to us. Well, I thought, we could buy it, if we can sell our house. It would be very convenient. We wouldn't have such a big place to look after and we wouldn't have to move very far. The only problem was that no one seemed to want to buy our house. We had had a couple of people come to look at it, but then nothing. Perhaps it was better to stay put with Bob's dementia. He might become even more confused if we moved.

***

At the end of January we went to the hospital again for the results of the endoscopy. I had been worrying so much but it was pretty good news. Bob had a small low grade cancerous tumour. They could remove it, but said that because of his age, it was unlikely to grow much and so they were just going to keep an eye on it. I decided I would look up natural remedies for prostate cancer on the internet. It was a great relief that it was not anything worse.

I wrote to Kira:

Dear Kira,

I'm just writing to say hello and I love you. How are you and Rosy and Angel? I hope you are all well and happy. Bob's cancer is not serious which is a great relief but I'm feeling sad because Quack died a couple of weeks ago... I wrote a poem to Quack which I enclose.

I'm going to China with my friend Helen on 25th March for 15 days. The summer house at the top of the garden is almost finished. I'm going to call it 'Rwle' which means 'Somewhere' in Welsh.

I often think of you all and hope to come down to Cornwall in May or June to see you.....

Love,

Mum xx

***

In February Bob was given 'Attendance Allowance' but it caused us to have an almighty row because he couldn't seem to understand that the money had been given to him to pay for the carers and the ready meals. He said he didn't need the carers and he didn't want the meals and that was that! But he always seemed to enjoy the meals. The trouble was that if I was out, he would forget to eat. He did get very frustrated with the carers though. They were good kind women but we had so many different ones. This meant they didn't know Bob and with his speech problem they couldn't always understand what he was trying to say, especially when they didn't know where things were.

"Stupid woman," he said to me one day. "She didn't know how to cut an apple up!"

"But Bobby, they do their best. They have to rush from one house to another and they don't seem to get paid very much and I bet they don't have much training. Perhaps no one has ever taught them how to cut apples. You could teach them."

He muttered something about bloody women and walked off.

I rang up social services and asked if there was any chance that we could have the same two or at most, three carers and not different ones all the time.

"Bob is getting very agitated and confused by the constant changes in carers."

After this they increased the number of hours he was having to six hours a week and we seemed to have fewer changes. I talked to my friend Frieda - ever a mine of information and help with her experience in caring for her friend Ray - and she told me to keep asking for more help as and when I needed it.

"As Bob gets worse he is entitled to more help but they don't always tell you what you are entitled to. The total number of hours he will eventually be entitled to is around thirty two hours a week, so keep asking."

"Thanks, Frieda."

***

A few days later Gillian came round and talked to Bob and made him see reason over his attendance allowance. He then did a direct debit into my account so I could pay for the meals etc. Bless Gillian; he always seemed to listen to her. I was so grateful for such a good friend.

At the time, social services seemed to deem Bob capable of managing his own money so it was too soon to take over his finances totally. If he was still able to sort out a direct debit with the bank I could hardly turn around and enforce the Power of

Attorney, could I? I decided he would feel so angry and betrayed if I did it too soon. However, I did manage a few weeks later to get his pin number for his debit card. I just asked him what it was and he told me. I wrote it down and decided I would only use it once he could no longer manage his affairs at all.

On February 14th Bobby gave me a Valentine's card again. He had written in it, but this year he didn't seem to have noticed the mistakes. I still have that card. It says above the card's words: 'you're the only one for me' "Ji just say ness" and then under the card's script: "as jo you, you - you are; you — a loving."

I gave him a great big hug. "Thank you Bobby, that's lovely!"

It seemed like only yesterday that he would never have given me a Valentine's card. He would more likely have written me a poem or some philosophical thoughts. But that person had gone and would never return and I still loved this person, though I hated intensely what was happening to him.

Over the month of February his ability to talk slowly but steadily declined. His ability to read and write was also slowly getting worse. Everyday tasks he sometimes coped with well and at other times his attempts to cope went crazily awry. For example, I came home one lunch time to find him with the head torch on his head. He thought it was night time and he was going out to shut the hens into their hutch for the night. Another day he seemed more his old self and did a perfectly lovely job of painting the window frame of the new summer house with varnish. I never knew what to expect from day to day.

One day we went on a great day out. We went to Chester on a coach trip with the Quakers to see the Quaker Tapestry in Chester Cathedral. The tapestry contained scenes from Quaker life and history and was interesting as well as beautifully hand stitched. It was a lovely day. The sun shone and Dafydd and his girlfriend Jenn came with us. After looking at the tapestry we walked along the ancient walls of the town and did a bit of window shopping too. Bob enjoyed seeing our Quaker friends and they were pleased to see us. It thoroughly perked him up. He was full of smiles and said a few words to everyone he met. It made me think that I must get out to the Quaker meeting with him more often. I hadn't been out walking on the mountains with him either, but then, the weather had been either wet or cold and he was not so sure footed as he used to be. It had been best to walk the lanes and along the beaches instead until the weather was better.

I did have a couple of nights away from Bob and he seemed to manage okay. I stayed at a friend's cottage for a sort of writing retreat making a start on my next writing project for the M.A. It was going to be a long poem but I'd started developing a different idea. It was to be a sort of monologue from the point of view of an old lady who was getting dementia. I thought that maybe writing it would help me to understand Bob better.

In those two days away, I had time to walk up into the mountains and time to think. I worried about Bob and my planned trip to China. If only I'd realised a few months back just how much worse Bob would be, I would never have booked the holiday with Helen. I needed to act on Bob's behalf if I was to go away at all. He needed more consistent help.

When I returned, I rang Bob's social worker and explained that he found it very confusing having different people coming to help him all the time and that I needed a better arrangement, especially as I was going to be away soon in China for two and a bit weeks. She then told me about the 'Direct Payment Scheme' where I could set up an account and Social Services would pay money into it, and I could then employ people to care for Bob.

"But you have to keep accounts so we can see how the money is being spent."

The Social worker sounded concerned.

"Well, that's not a problem as I do that with my own business."

I wished she'd told me about this 'Direct Payment Scheme' before. I then went on my computer and found out that I could have asked for a direct payment all along instead of having Bob's support arranged and paid for by the local Social Services.

So with very little time left I organized three different people to come in while I was away. Deb, my neighbour and Janet, who lived just down the road, were both people who Bob knew, and then I found another lady who was willing to fill in when they were not available. They would pop in and see him very regularly. They would help him get a meal for himself, check he had remembered to feed the hens and Heidi. I felt pretty sure he would be okay. Janet is into photography, as Bob is, so she said she'd do some photography with him. Deb said she'd get Bob to come out for walks with her and Jazz, the dog. The other lady would just pop in every evening to make sure that Bob had had his supper and shut the hens up. With all this planned I was still worried. I thought of cancelling the trip but then I would be letting Helen down. She was disabled and couldn't do the journey without me. I told myself not to worry. All would be well.

And then I went and had an almighty row with Bob...

It was his obsession with the keys. He was constantly locking and unlocking doors. He would pick up any keys that were lying around and put them in his pocket or hide them. He would lock the doors from the inside when we wanted to go out of them. What with this and him tiring me out waking me up every night, thinking it was time to get up I just suddenly lost my temper. I screamed and I shouted at him like a fish wife. I said "the fucking bloody keys!" over and over again. Then I said that I wished I'd never met him which was not true because I loved him. I just wished I could be free of the awful burden of looking after him. But really, after I'd calmed down I felt terrible... Poor Bob, he was the one with the illness. I said I was sorry but he just walked away and I couldn't blame him.

For a few days he hardly spoke to me, though I tried to be as loving as I could and told him that I was sorry. It was at times like this that I felt completely positive that he did not have Alzheimer's disease. He obviously remembered how horrible I had been to him. Someone with Alzheimer's would have forgotten because of the loss of short term memory. Bob did remember but he was not someone to hold anger forever. In the past we would have been able to talk about our problems. Now he could not speak very well and I think he did not always understand everything spoken, especially if it was a long sentence or a complex idea. We could still share his music though. I asked him if he would sing and he did and I played my piano. I sat beside him on the sofa and held his hand sometimes while I played some of his CDs. And then he held my hand again when we crossed the road in Caernarfon.

"Give us your paw" he said, just as he always had. He could still manage short phrases quite well.

***

Over the next week or so we became really close and loving again. I knew that I just had to treasure the best moments, the happy times between the difficult ones. With this in mind we were getting on so much better. We had a lovely Easter together. It was a wet day on Easter Sunday so we lazed in bed and ate Easter eggs like a couple of little kids. Bob wanted to read to me. He read a short story very, very slowly. It was a struggle but I wanted to encourage him to keep trying. He used to love reading out loud and was brilliant at it. He should have been an actor... the way he could change his voice for each character. I didn't want him to feel too distressed and down but then sometimes he'd realise just how little he could read now and he would look fearful.

"What's happening to me, Ali?"

I would just hug him then and fight back the tears. I didn't think that there was anything I could say that would make him feel better. He kept several pairs of glasses around him and would keep changing them over and often he'd blame them for his inability to read.

I knew I would have to look for a longer term solution over Bob's care using the direct payments scheme. I would need someone who would be happy to work at looking after Bob for at least six months or more. Janet only wanted to work until the end of April as her other work would take off then. Deb also worked with her outdoor activities and she would be too busy by the time I returned from China. Then I suddenly thought of our friend Pete. Pete had just retired from running the shop where I used to work. He had had therapy rooms above the shop where therapists could give treatments. Quite often Bob would pop into the shop when I was working there so he knew Pete and thought of him as a friend.

I rang him up immediately and Pete agreed to come on board as Bob's chief carer – apart from me that is. Pete said he was happy to work the full thirty two hours (when they eventually increased to that amount) so it was absolutely ideal! Pete liked to keep busy.

The first thing he said to me when I asked him if he'd like the job was:

"Well, as long as I can do things with Bob. You know me, Ali, I can't stand sitting around."

I just laughed, "That will be brilliant, Pete! That's just what Bob needs and also because he knows you, he'll not think of you as his carer but just his friend".

I told Pete how proud and independent Bob had always been and that if he felt he was being 'cared for' all the time he would hate it and probably become grumpy or even angry. I also told Pete how when I first started trying to get a bit of help in the early days and rang various bodies such as Age Concern, they said they could provide a few hours 'sitting service!'

"But Bob doesn't sit – well – not much. Can't you provide a 'walking or doing something' service?" They really didn't get it.

The day before our planned trip to China, Helen told me she was too ill to come with me. Poor Helen, she had been so looking forward to it. It was a package trip so there was no problem with me going on my own.

I phoned Bob just before I boarded the plane. He sounded fine. I just prayed that he wouldn't be too much trouble for Janet and Deb and the other lady. I'd arranged for them to drop in three times a day as he had been awarded more money. I just had to hope that all would go well while I was away.

I returned to Britain on 11th April. I had tried to phone Bob while I was away but he must have been out or asleep. I'd had a wonderful trip and seen many amazing things, like the Great Wall and the Terracotta Army, but that is part of another story.

***

Back in Britain, Helen and her husband, Alan, picked me up from the airport and I told them what a wonderful time I'd had. I hadn't been able to speak to Bob or anyone else while I'd been away.

I'd had a few tries, but no luck. Now Helen told me that Deb had rung her and said that Bob was a lot worse. Apparently he had been fine until about five days ago. Then he began to hallucinate. He said there were nasty goblin faced people in the house and that they were mocking him and doing rude things. Also he'd lost two sets of back door keys. Deb called in the police just in case these people were real. The policeman who came was called Michael and he was able to reassure Bob, Deb said.

I felt numb with worry. "I should never have gone away." I said to Helen.

When I got home I found a Bob who had a terrified look in his eyes. At first it was as if he didn't really register that I was home. He had just 'seen' these people again. He asked me over and over,

"What's happening to me, Ali?" I didn't know what to say to him. I held his hands and kissed his face.

"I don't know my Bobby, I don't know."

I was very tired and jet-lagged and still had a bad chesty cough that I'd caught in Beijing so I just kept falling asleep. I didn't know what to do about my Bob so I just kept hugging him and holding his hand and playing his favourite music. I gave him some reflexology to help him relax and massaged his shoulders. I took him out as much as possible. We went down to the sea and bought ice creams at the shop and sat on a bench and watched the waves. I still wasn't very well. So I went to see the doctor. He checked my chesty cough and said it wasn't serious. While I was there I asked him about Bob and his hallucinations. He said there was some medicine he could take which might help but he probably needed to go back to Dr Kurian at the hospital.

Later Bob and I went to see Gillian and she gave us both a massage which helped my jet lag and cough and calmed Bob. He didn't have any more hallucinations for a while after that.

***

At the beginning of May, I went down to Cornwall for a few days as it was Rosy and Amber's birthdays. Pete looked after Bob while I was away and I was so grateful to him. He was an answer to a prayer and he and Bob worked well together. He got Bob to help him with all sorts of jobs around the house and garden.

In the middle of May we went to see the neurologist and unfortunately it was a waste of his time and ours. I had been hoping he could shed more light on Bob's condition and we had been waiting for several months for this appointment. We drove to Bangor and waited for an hour in the waiting room. When we finally saw him it was only to be told that without more information from Doctor Kurian he couldn't do anything. I was a bit dumbfounded that Doctor Kurian had not sent him any details of Bob's condition. The neurologist angrily waved a letter at us which he said didn't explain anything. After two minutes we were dismissed so we went to the hospital café for coffee and buns to cheer ourselves up before we went home.

A week later, I went down with a tummy bug and so did Bob. Fortunately it was just a 24 hour thing that was going around.

The next day we went to see Dr Kurian. He explained that he wanted to conduct an experiment with Bob with my help. So together we spent time trying to see if Bob could remember things from the previous few days, especially interesting or unusual things. It was obvious that Bob did. He couldn't find all the words... I suggested Cwm Pennant where we'd been two days ago.

We'd had a lovely day out. We'd walked up to the old ruined house that Bob always loved to visit and had sat for a while looking at the view and the birds in the trees. There were new-born lambs playing in the fields and a herd of cows came up to the fence as we wandered back to the car... I asked Bob to remember that day.

He managed to convey "somewhere beautiful with cows... small animals... birds", but he didn't seem to remember or maybe could not find the words to say that he'd been sick yesterday but just said that there'd been "a lot of sitting around yesterday". Dr Kurian and I worked together with these specific questions.

Afterwards, he said that he was sure that Bob didn't have any normal recognisable dementia like Alzheimer's. He said Bob obviously had some memory loss, but the biggest loss was that of language and that would obviously impact on his memory as we use language to hold information together in our brains.

I then told Dr Kurian that I felt a bit annoyed that he hadn't sent any details of Bob's condition to the neurologist, but he said that he'd written a letter and that was all he normally did unless he was asked to give more information. So it was obviously a lack of communication between the two departments. I thought that maybe I should complain more but it wouldn't help Bob. Maybe it might help others, I thought, but then I was feeling so overwhelmed with how much worse Bob was that I really didn't have the energy to complain anyway.

I then said that Bob was having hallucinations and that I was worried about them but Dr Kurian didn't seem concerned about Bob's hallucinations at all.

In fact he was rather dismissive. Perhaps it was because I'd said they seemed to only happen occasionally, though when they did, I told him, I found them scary. I wanted to talk to Dr Kurian about the hallucinations in more detail but he looked at his watch. He had other people to see. I should have spoken up. Maybe I should have demanded more advice but he was not going to give us any more time. I felt very frustrated but I was tired from having had a tummy bug the day before so there was no fight left in me. We said goodbye and left.

***

At the end of May I went away to friends for a couple of nights and came back to find that Bob had woken Andy and Deb up at 4 a.m. I was very upset to hear this. Pete had been with him during the day but I thought he would be okay to be left at night. "If I have to go away again", I thought to myself, "I'll have to ask Pete if he wouldn't mind staying overnight".

Over and over again I had tried to explain to Bob about time but nothing I did seemed to make any difference. I asked him about waking Andy and Deb but he just got angry and stomped off and wouldn't speak to me.

Fortunately, Bob liked Pete and said, "He's a very nice man".

Pete had been getting him to chop up wood for the stove and Bob now said that he wanted to be paid for the wood he'd been chopping! Dear Lord, it was his stove as well as mine! But he didn't understand and I found it so hard to accept this.

I could get money to pay for Pete to care for him, but because I lived in the same house and had my pension now, I couldn't claim a carer's allowance for me. I was rapidly cutting back on all my work as I had to look after him so much more and had found another local chiropodist to take over some of the clientele.

Suddenly it seemed I was going to be quite hard up, but Bob hardly spent any of his pension. He thought he was hard up because he only had a few pounds in his purse. He would often sit in his chair and empty his purse. He then made little piles of money on the arm of his chair and counted it up.

"I have hardly any money."

"But Bob, you've plenty of money in the bank."

"No I don't."

"Look, let me show you."

So I would go and get his bank statements but he didn't believe them. He had thousands of pounds in there. He then

145

always demanded that we call in at the bank for a fresh statement when we were in Caernarfon. Then he'd stare at the paper they gave him. I don't think he really understood how to read a statement anymore.

"What's this mean?" He'd asked the cashier. They'd explain it carefully to him and were all so patient with him. The little Indian lady was his favourite and she was particularly kind to him.

"Hello Mr Treves." She would always say. "How are you today?"

"Very well thank you," he'd answer "and how are you?"

Then she would ask: "And what can I do for you today?"

I really don't know how many times he went to the bank to ask for a bank statement, but they never complained. They would print it out for him and carefully explain to him what it meant, over and over and over again. Years later, long after Bob had died, I met the little Indian lady again. She was working in another bank.

"How is Mr Treves?" she asked.

"Unfortunately he passed away." I answered.

"Oh I'm so sorry to hear that," she said. "He was such a nice man. We all liked him."

***

Bob's moods went up and down but for quite some time he had very few hallucinations and when he did they weren't so unpleasant. He didn't see the horrible goblin type people who had frightened and upset him. He did see some people on horseback going across a field once. The field looked empty to me, but he said that they looked like soldiers. Sometimes a person would sit on the sofa next to me. Bob said she was a woman and that she hadn't been invited into our house. He would sound annoyed but not frightened. I would turn to the empty seat next to me and politely but firmly ask her to leave. Bob would then seem happy that she had gone so I felt I was doing the right thing.

I think that his mind was helped by the constant exercise of sawing wood and chopping it up into smaller pieces with an axe.

He'd always said in the past that hard physical work helped to focus his mind. It had become an obsession but there was no harm in it. It got him out into the fresh air and he enjoyed it. I did try vainly to get him to saw the wood on the Black and Decker workmate but he insisted on using what had been a quite nice garden table. He regularly misjudged the depth and size of the wood he was cutting, so the table had slits and cuts all over it.

When it came to chopping I tried to persuade him that it would be a good idea to chop onto a larger block of wood but no, the chopping had to be done straight down onto the patio slabs. So the garden table was full of cuts and I had several broken patio slabs but what the heck. His happiness was more important to me, and him not having horrible hallucinations was more important than garden tables and patio slabs. Sooner or later something different or worse would happen. I had to just survive each day and try not to be upset or have any expectations.

Every day brought new challenges as Bob's condition worsened. The disturbed nights went from about 3-4 nights a week to nearly every night. The doctor gave him sleeping tablets but they made no difference. He would regularly wake me up at 4 a.m. or earlier and wouldn't go to bed till gone 11 p.m. More and more he would get all his clothes in a muddle, often putting clothes on in the wrong order, like underpants on top of trousers.

"Why can't I pee?" He said to me one morning. Somehow he'd put his jeans on back to front!

Sometimes he would forget how to make a cup of tea or coffee or forget how to put the TV on or work the CD player. Other times he would remember. Sometimes he would turn the cooker and the gas on when we weren't cooking anything. I had to rescue the food in the freezer when he turned that off. (After that episode I taped the freezer switch down in the on position and tried to hide the switch under a tea towel). He was constantly hiding or losing the keys so I now kept some of them well hidden in a box in the bottom drawer in the utility room and the rest in a zipped pocket of a jacket hidden under other jackets.

I liked to get him to do things to help so I would ask him to cut up the fruit for breakfast but now I had to watch what he was doing otherwise we would end up eating orange peel and apple cores and the good bits would go in the hen bowl. The hens were delighted I'm sure, but I wasn't! Then if I didn't hang onto my breakfast bowl, I would sometimes find he'd eaten mine as well as his own. Poor Heidi was also very confused by his odd behaviour. He took to locking the cat flap so she was either locked out or locked in. I would sometimes wake to hear her plaintive meows in the middle of the night.

***

The social worker and social services people were coming to see us and I needed to persuade them to give me more hours. I wrote down a list of all these new problems I was having so that they would have it in black and white. I needed to make it clear to them that I was finding looking after Bob very challenging – to put it mildly! Just before they arrived for the meeting I found he'd put his razor and toothbrush in the cutlery drawer and his alarm clock in the fridge.

"It would be funny if it wasn't so exhausting!" I told them when they arrived. "I gave him a simple job to do the other day when he said he wanted to help. "Could you take the washing off the line please?" I said. I gave him the peg bag and he disappeared up the garden. Half an hour later he hadn't come back so I went out to see what he was doing. Guess what? I had to laugh. He was making a beautiful arrangement of pegs all along the washing line in different coloured patterns. I smiled and said. "Well, that's lovely!" We did get the washing in eventually."

After this meeting social services did increase Bob's hours to seventeen a week. I would have liked more but perhaps I should have shown them more desperation and less humour...

Chapter 8

Free Fall

The Facts Are These (in 2008)

The lowest paid welfare benefit is carer's allowance

but if your carer who you live with

has a state pension she can't have carer's allowance

But if she lives somewhere else she can be paid to look after you

maybe six or more pounds an hour

If you are over 65 you can't have disability living allowance

but you can have attendance allowance

and a little top up on your pension for your disability

don't get it wrong

you do get something which is almost £500 a month

but

the government hopes you won't be abandoned by the one you

love

she will give up a good job to look after you night and day

an unpaid nurse

learning as she goes slightly

crazy

and yes there are social workers out there

and they try their best

but they have their rules

and when she really needs them they are sick or on holiday or

out on another case

and when your carer

asks and asks they tell her that you could be having this or that

and did they not tell her

they probably did

not

then other helpers come

they are not bad

some are angels without wings

and when your carer asks for more

and yes there's more but only 32 hours a week out of 168

or you can pay a lot of cash to agencies

and after that there's always respite care

a week or two at a residential home

you'll have to go eventually for good

you cry

no

you want to stay

you cannot help this bloody thing
you try your best to be a help and
know they think that you are daft
and you just want your old self back

you hear behind closed doors
he's getting worse
and you are frightened
do not mean to be a burden but
just want familiar faces and to stay at home

The next few months were exhausting. I quickly realised I would have to stop working all together. Several times, I nearly fell asleep at the wheel of the car on the way to or from visiting a patient... With Bob waking up two or three or sometimes even four times a night, I would be lucky if I got four hours sleep, often it was two. The stress of never knowing what he would get up to if he woke and I wasn't there to check on him meant that even when I slept I became like a dog with one ear cocked, ready to wake at the slightest sound. If I did not wake straight away, I would often find him trying to get dressed with six socks on one foot and none on the other, or his underpants on top of his trousers and he, knowing something was wrong but not able to put it right, would be so frustrated and angry.

I would attempt to calm him by massaging his shoulders and his feet. It might take me an hour or so to persuade him to go back to bed. Other times he would go downstairs and start trying to prepare food or cook. Once or twice, I woke to find that every single vegetable and piece of fruit in the kitchen was cut into tiny pieces. I tried giving him some valerian and skullcap tablets and they did seem to help for a little while. I took him to the doctor and a blood test revealed that his vitamin B12 was low so he had a course of injections but it didn't seem to make much difference. The doctor also gave me some stronger sleeping tablets and I gave him those sometimes but only if I was desperate. I really didn't like drugs like those and they didn't always make much difference anyway.

Then, during the day he would sometimes disappear for a long while and would turn up having got a bus to Caernarfon and then walked home or he'd take one of the many local footpaths around our hamlet and arrive home muddy and/or damp. I'd have the added worry of not knowing where he was, but I found that his ability to find his way around didn't seem to be affected by his type of dementia. There was no way I could stop a big strong six foot man from going wherever he wanted anyway. So then I'd hope that he would sleep after a long walk but it seemed to make no difference at all.

Sometimes I would call my younger daughter, Alexis. She was good to talk to and often would cheer me up by just being her funny cheerful self.

In June I took Bob to see a healer who my friend Helen had recommended. She was a lovely person and Bob seemed much taken with her but she was also very honest.

"There is really nothing much I can do for him," she confessed, "apart from helping him to feel calmer for a short while."

I realised I was clutching at every straw that came my way, looking for, longing for a miracle. But there were no miracles for Bob. I needed to stop hurting myself by hoping.

***

Around this time I gave up work completely apart from doing a little reflexology. Every day Bob seemed to be getting worse and I just simply could not continue. I never knew what he was going to do next and my head and my nerves felt scrambled. So I rang each patient up and said goodbye.

I - dot,
blade of grass
waving
uselessly.

He restlessly
pacing earth
brain going
going,
day on day,
hour on hour,
dots getting dottier.

There's no sense,
wind or rain
just this pain
snarled,
gnarled,
a sick joke.

My chiropody career had ended. I felt as though my relationship with Bob had pretty nigh ended too.

I blew my top at him one night. He wouldn't take the herbal tablets that helped him sleep. I'd only had two hours sleep the night before because he got up three times. I couldn't rest much during the next day as we both had dental appointments and shopping to do and I was exhausted. I told him if he wouldn't take them then I was leaving. I went and got my bedding and the camper van keys but he barred my way and told me not to be stupid. I threw the box of tablets on the floor and they went everywhere. I wanted to run away from this man that I loved but who was no longer the person he had been. Dear God, was I just too weak?

Gillian had been learning aromatherapy and had been practicing on me and Bob. It was a great help – so relaxing and calming. Then she took her practical exam and I was invited to be one of the 'bodies.' It meant I had two massages in three days and I felt so much better. Pete stayed at our house and looked after Bob. He got Bob to 'help' fix our trailer. Good old Pete!

I told him, "You're an angel without the wings."

He laughed "I'm no angel".

Also one of the local residential homes, Plas Maesincla, (where I used to work doing chiropody on the residents feet) said they would look after Bob for the odd half day. That was good news. Then social services increased Bob's attendance allowance hours to 23... so I had good news all round!

It was nearly the end of July and Bob was still working away at sawing wood and chopping it into tiny pieces for kindling. I'd tried again to persuade him to use the workbench and not the garden table. I'd also asked him please, to not cut it up so small. We now had enough kindling to last about a year or two and then two days later the garden table finally bit the dust. Bob cut it in half! With life as it was I just laughed and got the Black and Decker workbench out but he just stomped off. After that he didn't cut any more wood.

***

August came and I drove to Cornwall and brought all three grandchildren back to Wales. Pete was brilliant and stayed overnight while I was away. Bob was happy to see the children and on the whole the week went well though my grandchildren were far easier to manage than Bob!

It rained like the monsoon most days but we had lots of fun. We went to the beach, we went to the woods. We splashed in puddles and got muddy and wet but nobody cared. I just put things in the washing machine and the children in the bath.

One day we walked along the lake to a beautiful secret place I knew and the children made fairy houses out of moss and sticks. Bob came too but he was a bit of a pain worrying over the children being so close to the waterfall. We had a little picnic of fruit and biscuits and then went down to the lake. I had a swim and the children played and swam and then sat on the gravel and gave themselves gravelly bums. It was a day to remember.

***

Bob was very difficult and at times, a total grump. I felt he was struggling, trying to be the old Bobby who my grandchildren knew and loved, trying and failing to be his old self. Once or twice he got angry because the children didn't understand what he was telling them. They were frightened by his anger but they were also wonderfully patient with him too. His speech was very up and down. Sometimes he just made sounds that made no sense, other times he could say things quite clearly. But I was just so happy to have all my grandchildren together again that I was not going to let anything spoil this wonderful time.

On the last day, when it rained all day long, my neighbour Deb came over and helped the children make all sorts of crazy things out of cardboard boxes, glue and sellotape while I caught up on some sleep before the long drive all the way back to Cornwall.

***

I was often very tired but whenever I could I would walk alone up into the mountains or into the woods or if there was very little time, I would just wander up to my summer house. I had a beautiful view of the mountains from there. Being and walking quietly in nature was a great balm. Often I wrote my thoughts and feelings down into to my diary or into my work for my M.A. I had finished writing the monologue of the old lady with dementia and my tutors were very pleased with it. One day I wrote in my diary:

"I'm sitting up on a hillside watching a buzzard and hearing its high lonely mournful cry. 'Ee -ee - pee - eppee.' I feel like the bird song: lonely and mournful at the thought that my Bob will most probably have to go into a home before too long and despite all the difficulties I shall miss him so very much."

Towards the end of August Bob's hallucinations came back with a vengeance.

"They are horrible." Bob kept saying, though he was never really able to explain in what way they were horrible. They frightened and angered him. It was awful. Bob was suddenly so angry and so difficult. He kept shouting at these 'people' and throwing things at them. One day, while I was out, one of our neighbours found him running across the fields near her house with a kitchen knife in his hand. He said he was chasing some of the bad people who had come into the house. She, like all our neighbours, was wonderful with him. She said that the bad people had gone now and would he like a cup of tea.

"Yes please," said Bob. So she took him home and they had a nice cuppa at her house. He forgot about the knife so she put it in her pocket and walked home with him. Apparently there was a half cut slice of bread on the work surface so she just put the bread away and the knife in the drawer.

Every day now he would throw cushions at these bad people and I had to pretend that I could see them too. I'd look into thin air and speak sternly.

"Get out of our house," I would say, "you don't belong here!"

Deb saw me doing this and she said that she thought I shouldn't pretend I could see them, but they were obviously so real to Bob and it was the only way to calm him down. He couldn't rest. One night, he was constantly seeing the people... strange rude beings in the house and outside and was so frightened that he hardly slept and so I hardly slept either. In the morning we went to the doctor's surgery. We had a long wait because everyone wanted to see our doctor. When we finally got in to see him and I explained what was happening, he was very kind and sympathetic. He rang the specialist, Dr Kurian, at the hospital. Yes, there was some medication he could take and we were to call back this afternoon to pick it up.

***

We then drove to Plas Maesincla where Bob was to spend some of the day. The staff could see how worn out I was and said to go home and rest. I did a bit of shopping and went home but had no chance to rest. Plas Maessincla rang to say that Bob was getting very agitated, so could I come back. They also rang Bob's social worker, Angharad, and she phoned me to say she was arranging a bed at the Heulwen dementia ward, in Ysbyty Gwynedd hospital for him to be assessed that night. I told her that it all felt too much, too soon. I was not ready to give up on Bob. I told her, "I know I need a break but I have picked up the tablets from the surgery and I would like to see if they make things better first."

A few days later I wrote her a report of the situation in the hopes that they would increase the hours I received to help with Bob's care. This is a copy of it:

Notes on Robert Treves, for the form "Assessing your needs as a carer."

Re section 3
General overview

At the moment Bob has Direct Payments of 17 hours a week and I have 6 hours... so 23 altogether. This had seemed quite adequate when Angharad proposed it to me a few months ago. However

Bob's condition has worsened and his behaviour has become so difficult that by the last 10 days I have felt ready to give up. I know he would find it very difficult to be locked up in a home, so now that he is on Seroquel, which is making him calmer with fewer hallucinations, I *am* willing to try to continue looking after him, but only if I can have more help.

In detail

I often have to give up trying to sleep by 5-6 a.m. and get up and give him his breakfast and his tablets. These have to be hidden, crushed and put in a honey sandwich as he refuses to swallow them and will angrily spit them out. He often has difficulty dressing, e.g. puts 4 socks on one foot, and his shirt on top of his sweater. Often he takes all his clothes out of the drawers and muddles up the clean and dirty clothes. He often loses his false teeth, or his comb or his wallet, etc... He often needs to be reminded to wash properly. Nowadays he refuses to ever have a bath. If he is in a good enough mood he will do his knee exercises as suggested by the physiotherapist, but only with my help.

After this he will either sit in his chair and fall asleep, or wander around the house 'helping.' This might consist of repeatedly washing up the dishes, e.g. the same bowl 3-4 times, putting things away in all sorts of odd places so I have to go around finding/collecting things. He constantly needs reassurance about all sorts of things. He gets upset because he does not understand about money anymore. I have to explain the same thing over and over again and he still does not understand. Often I cannot find out what the problem is because he cannot find the right words and so I try to change the subject or get him to listen to some of his favourite music or a TV programme he enjoys. Sometimes he will settle down on his own for a short while, but usually within 20 minutes he will call me needing help(unless he's fallen asleep).

He can no longer operate the CD player or the TV. He can no longer read or write much. He often breaks things and he often gets alarmed because he's 'seen' someone who is not really there, and usually this makes him angry. He does all sorts of silly things if I am not constantly watching him. He cannot make himself a drink unless he is just pouring a glass of water or fruit juice. I don't let him try to do any cooking, it's too dangerous, though he does still like to help me cut up fruit and veg. I find this a bit nerve racking, but he is happiest when he feels he is 'helping.'

Usually either I or Peter take him out either for a walk or a drive in the car or to 'help' in the garden. He's happiest when out and about, especially meeting other people, but he has on several occasions gone off on his own without saying and has had to be found.

In the evening I will cook him a meal and we generally watch TV or listen to music. He will not settle for long unless I watch or listen with him. I try to keep him awake so he will sleep better later. But there is no guaranteed way to insure I have a good night's sleep and am grateful for the nights when he does sleep through. Often I end up with only 2-3 hours of sleep. The sleeping tablets have very little effect, but he is slightly better with the seroquel.

To sum up and re section 10

1. His ability to talk is getting far worse
2. His moods are getting far worse. He's never physically aggressive, but verbally, he can be very frightening and I often find myself shaking and crying.

3. Before he started these new tablets he was chasing people he 'saw' away, once with a big kitchen knife. He still does see them and last night (Saturday), he had a bad turn, running around the garden in the pouring rain, moving all my flower pots and chasing these 'People' and getting very agitated and wet. I'm afraid this sort of behaviour totally freaks me out. I think it's the strange

terrified look in his eyes, like he's possessed. So I think they will have to increase the dose. (It is under review.)

4. He tips tea and coffee down himself very often, so I have a lot more washing to do.

5. I need to carry on working and doing my courses. I need the money and I need to keep sane. At the moment I sometimes feel I am no longer sane. I get so tired and then get angry and upset. I also need to visit my family in Cornwall and help with my grandchildren.

6. **Therefore I need Bob's support time to be increased to at least 4 hours a day, plus the 6 hours for me, if possible. I don't think he is safe to be left for any length of time at all now.**

I would also like him to spend some time in respite, maybe when I have a weekend course, or go to Cornwall to help my family or just for the odd day so I can catch up on some much needed sleep. I am waiting to see how settled he will be on these new tablets as he will not settle at Plas Maesincla at the moment. The first time he got very angry at being locked in (he hates any authority stopping him from doing what he wants to do and always has). The second time, the only way I could get him to settle for the afternoon, was to stay with him (they kindly found me somewhere to sleep).

Commitments in Detail

These are variable, but generally are as follows. These times include travelling time as I do not feel Bob should be left on his own for very long.

Monday
Aprox 6 hours: Reflexology and course work for my M.A.

Tuesday
Aprox 8 hours: Reflexology, course work and lecture in Bangor

Wednesday
Aprox 3 hours: Welsh class and 2 and a half hours Yoga.

Thursday
Aprox 4 hours: Welsh Class and work in Caernarfon

Friday
Welsh conversation class 2-3 hours

Saturday and Sunday
I have about one course a month I need to go on. Some of these are local, some residential. 7 – 10 hours approx.

Total approx. 34 hours a week.

After this report they did give me the full thirty two hours of help. This sounds a lot until you remember that there are 168 hours in a week.

***

A while ago I had bought tickets for Bob and I to go to the Opera Gala at the Faenol festival. He loved going so much and would probably never go again. Gillian and Holger hadn't planned to go this year but at the last moment Gillian, bless her, said she would come to help me look after Bob.

The Opera Gala went fine and Bob enjoyed it thoroughly but I hardly took the music in. I was so tired and worried he might be difficult. Gillian was a gem for just being there. Bob called out "Bravo!" with great gusto as the end of every single aria and song. He really had lost a lot of his inhibitions. Before we went onto the field we had to queue and Gillian helped me not to lose him in the crowds and once we had settled ourselves, she stayed with him while I went to the toilet.

At half time he went to the toilet himself. I followed him to make sure he didn't get lost. Then he enjoyed the picnic I had brought but I had to hide some of the cake Gillian had brought otherwise he would have eaten it all and left none for us! I was so grateful to her and on the way home I offered to pay for her ticket. After I'd dropped her off though, Bob started being very verbally aggressive. I knew it was the dementia talking and not his old self.

He had become so very fixated on money. He said Gillian should pay for her *own* ticket. I felt he was driving me mad. He never used to be like this. I would have given all the money in the world for him to be better and here he was, getting angry over the price of a ticket. I had to bite my tongue and remind myself that this was just the dementia talking.

When we got home I crushed his sleeping tablet and the new tablets and put them in a honey sandwich. It was the only way to get tablets into him... ...and then took a sleeping tablet myself, something I would never normally do, but I so needed to sleep. I thought to myself, "I have so many tablets here... if I was the suicidal type I could polish them all off and just not wake up'" - but I would never, ever have done that. I was not into suicide or into giving up, not on Bob and not on myself.

Soon Bob was a whole lot better so I was pretty sure that the seroquel tablets were helping. He had not had even one hallucination for two whole days and he was sleeping a little better. Then Bob's old friend Jan phoned to ask if she could come and stay soon? She was also visiting a friend in Tywyn. I thought to myself, "I wish she had come a year or so ago when Bob was more his old self", but I was glad she was coming. She and Bob had always been very fond of each other. Her visit would do him good. She was one of his best friends. Also Bob seemed more 'on the ball' with the tablets but he did still frequently wake me after I'd only had three or four hours sleep. I had to catch up on my sleep whenever Pete came to help or doze on a sofa at Plas Maesincla while he was being looked after there.

***

At the beginning of September I went to see the solicitor. It was time to bite the bullet and take full charge of Bob's affairs with the 'Power of Attorney' that we set up a while ago. I hadn't done it any sooner because with Bob's obsession with money and going to the bank for bank statements I was afraid that he would feel betrayed if I took control. After all he had been trying in his own way to maintain some sort of control. But now he was so much worse he seemed to have let go of this obsession with going to the bank. Perhaps it was the tablets. They certainly were helping him to be more relaxed. The only bad side effect of the tablets was an increase in appetite and weight gain, but at least he was now more contented.

***

One day we went to see some old friends from Quakers, Flora and Roy, and had a lovely day with them. We had a walk on the beach and then lunch at their house. Bob's speech was getting even more slurred and Roy and Flora had difficulty understanding him but they were wonderfully patient with him. Then he tried to eat his soup with a knife and fork. Flora and Roy smiled and said nothing and I gently gave him the spoon instead.

Later, when we got home, we took Jazz for a walk and then Bob got into a mood about money again. He thought people were stealing his money. This obsession was not as bad as it had been but I suppose, if he had understood what I was doing, he would see my using his debit card to pay for things as stealing. I now had the Court of Protection's permission to manage his money but I was being very careful to keep account of what I spent. I had to pay for Pete's work caring for Bob, half the cost of the car, food, outings and his clothes. I needed to keep the money in his bank account below a certain figure otherwise when he did have to go into a home they would only take it off him to pay the expenses. So I decided that we should do something that he would really love and go to an opera in Llandudno and stay at a Bed and Breakfast somewhere nearby.

I bought tickets for Tosca and then looked for a sympathetic B&B. I found one – the lady said her mother had dementia. If it went to plan, I decided I would take Bob again while he was still well enough. The tablets were still making him put on weight but he was not hallucinating so much and was so much calmer. I wrote in my diary:

"Our trip to the opera went really well. The stay at the B & B went well too, though I was very nervous that Bob might get up and wake the whole household so I had a honey sandwich with his medication crushed up in it all ready when we got back to the room. He loves bread and honey so much. He always just woofs it down and doesn't notice it's got crushed pills in it. He did get up a couple of times and I got up too to just guide him into the en-suite bathroom and make sure he did not go out the door!

The lady who owns the B & B was very understanding so I shall definitely go there again if Bob is still well enough.

At the moment he's sitting and listening to an opera on his CD player and singing away to it. It's good to see him so happy. These pills are helping brilliantly and I'm getting more sleep too. Wonderful!"

***

In mid-September Jan came to stay for about two days and I drove all over the place in 'Charlie' our old campervan. Everything went well. Bob was so happy to see her. She wanted to go to places she remembered from her university days in Bangor, so we drove all over the mountains and went into Bangor for tea on the Bangor pier which she was thrilled with. In her student days it was an unsafe crumbling wreck. Since then it had been beautifully restored.

The next day we all went on the train from Porthmadog to Tywyn and wandered on the beach with her friend until it was time to say goodbye and get the train back.

Jan's visit to North Wales

Years later, Jan spoke of two abiding memories she had of her brief stay with us.

"On the first evening, Bob and I wandered along the lane to watch the sun go down over the sea. It was a beautiful sunset and we stood and watched the changing light and the movement of colours in the sky. Bob obviously wanted to say something about how beautiful it was. His words made little sense but I knew by the expression on his face roughly what he was trying to say. So I smiled and said a few words but we understood each other mainly by our facial expressions."

The other memory was of the trip to Bangor pier.
"Bob needed to go to the toilet and when he came out of the gents, I could see he was confused for a moment. Maybe he wasn't sure where he was but I saw fear in his eyes. Maybe it was a moment of clarity, of a realisation of the awfulness of his illness, I don't know.

'Oh Jesus!' he said and then he saw us and smiled and looked happy again."

I found Jan's memories very comforting and affirming. They helped me to realise that I was not alone in seeing how Bob suffered when he momentarily realised the awfulness of what was happening to him but how on the other hand he never lost his appreciation of the beauty of nature.

***

Unfortunately, after doing so much driving and with no power steering on the old Campervan, I somehow managed to strain my arm.

A few days later my arm was still extremely sore so I went to the acupuncturist in the hope she could help. While I was sitting in the waiting room I suddenly remembered that it was my birthday! I thought to myself. "Everyone has forgotten", so I sent a jokey text to Alexis: "Happy birthday to me???" She replied: "Oh Mum. Sorry I forgot. I will send you a card and a present soon! Lots of love xxx." I smiled to myself when I got her text as Alexis forgets every year so it's become a joke between us. She always remembers eventually.

Bob was more difficult after Jan went. He had always been

better when other people, especially friends, were around. Pete needed to have some time off work because of a family crisis so with the help of Bob's social worker, I arranged for Bob to go into a residential home on Anglesey for about a week and Pete promised to take him there as with such a sore arm it was very difficult for me to drive.

I remember it felt very strange without Bob but I was so exhausted with the pain in my arm and the need to catch up on months of sleep I just stayed in bed mostly. I thought a lot... and dreamt a lot, remembering how Bob used to be. The intellectual stimulus of having the most amazing and interesting discussions, the loving, wonderful sex we had had, and the fun of doing things together, working on the house or in the garden and walking on the mountains and by the sea.

He had always been someone who I could talk to about almost everything and anything. He was someone who had loved me like no other. He had shown me unconditional love. I had sometimes behaved very badly and he had seen the worst bits of me, but he had always forgiven me. I knew I probably had failed to love him as much as he loved me. I knew that such love is rare and that I was truly blessed to have been loved so much.

I lay there in bed, with tears in my eyes blessing him and so wishing that he could be well again. "There are still so many things I would have liked for us to do together but now will never do." I thought to myself. "Perhaps we can do those things in heaven..." I told my neighbour about my thoughts on heaven and he told me about the 'Near Death' experience he'd had as a young man when he nearly died from sepsis.

**

I tried writing in my diary but I couldn't write much with my left hand (I'm left-handed) as the arm was so sore, so I wrote with the other hand. It was very slow and wobbly.

After a few days I tried to drive but it hurt my arm so I got the bus into town and went to have my hair done. I rang the residential home and they said that Bob was happy. When Pete took him in, he had been very angry when he realised he was staying there but the lady I spoke to said he was getting on very well and was no trouble. In fact, she said, they were having a laugh and a joke with him. I hoped it was true. Pete and I would be fetching Bob on the Monday afternoon and I was feeling better every day. The day before we picked Bob up, Gillian gave me one of her wonderful aromatherapy massages and I slept like a babe.

With Bob back home after the break I found it hard to get back into looking after him but after a couple of days it was as if he'd never been away. I thought he looked older and gentler. It was probably the medication.

***

At the beginning of October, Pete, Bob and I went to see a speech therapist called Dawn. She was a lovely girl with big brown caring eyes. I was explaining to her how Bob's ability to talk had gradually declined, when suddenly he burst into deep, deep sobs. It was the first time he'd cried for about eighteen years, to my knowledge, and in the middle of his sobs he said that the residential home he'd stayed in was 'awful'. I didn't realise that he thought it was awful. He'd seemed happy enough when we went to pick him up. Maybe he also cried because I was describing to Dawn how he had lost his amazing ability with language. Maybe he suddenly realised what he had lost.

This is what made his type of dementia all the more cruel. It's not like Altzheimer's disease where memory is the first thing to be affected. With this frontal lobe type of vascular dementia it is speech that is the first thing to be affected, or so it had been in Bob's case. I'd never seen him sob like this, his whole body shook.

Dawn was so kind and sympathetic. I didn't know what to do. I gently stroked Bob's hand and hugged him.

Later, I thought about what my friend Frieda had said to me, that some homes pretend to be better than they truly are. I hoped it was just some aspects of that home that were awful as I was hoping he could have another week there in November. But I didn't want him to go somewhere he thought was awful.

***

During October Gillian was running a short course. It was about living in tune with nature and the earth and was called 'Earth Walking'. I decided to go on it. I felt it would be uplifting and refresh my flagging energies. It meant having a day and a night away from Bob, but Pete was happy to look after him. I would leave sometime Saturday morning and come home on Sunday afternoon. On the morning I was leaving, with Bob having been up and down in the night I gave him his breakfast early, at 7:00 a.m.

"Bobby," I said, "Pete is coming and will be staying here tonight. I'm going on a course and I'll be back tomorrow. I hope that's okay?"

"Yes," he said, but maybe I had given him too much information all at once. Maybe I should have talked about it the night before or maybe I should have repeated what I said.

Dawn had tried to explain that I needed to keep my sentences very short in order for him to understand now that his speech and understanding of speech was declining so fast.

I left about 8:30 and drove through the mountains to our friends near Crafnant where it was being held. It was a beautiful morning with mist coming and going and the sun breaking through the curtains of cloud. I was feeling tired but was really looking forward to the weekend.

Later in the day, Pete tried to phone me but there was no signal in the house and so it wasn't until I walked up the lane a little later that I found out he'd phoned. I phoned back and Pete told me that Bob had thrown a wobbly when he realised I wasn't coming home that night. Obviously he hadn't listened to me or hadn't understood when I'd explained I'd be away.

"Bobby," I said when Pete put him on. "I'm so sorry but I can't come home tonight. I'm on a course. I'm coming home tomorrow."

"You never told me", he said grumpily.

"I did tell you Bobby. I'm sorry... maybe you weren't listening."

"Well when... are you...?" He couldn't find the words.

"I'll be home tomorrow, my love. I'll see you in the afternoon. Please be nice to Pete and don't shout at him. It's not his fault. He's a nice man."

"Yes... he's not so nice now."

"Well, you be nice to him and then he'll be nice to you, please Bobby."

"Okay, okay... bloody women," he muttered.

"Night-night, sleep well. And see you tomorrow..."

"See you ...to... mmm."

I felt upset. I realised that probably I should have told Bob several times. As his condition worsened he didn't always understand. And then I felt cross and thought. "Do I have to be really ill to justify to myself and to others that I need a break from him? I feel I want to keep going, looking after him for as long as I can but I have to have time away otherwise I will crack up. I don't want to abandon him in a residential home for good until I'm really ill... But I don't want to get really ill. Oh shit! I'm not going to feel depressed. I'm going to enjoy the rest of this course whatever!"

***

Time passed and Bob continued to become more and more difficult. I rarely got much sleep. I tried not to lose my temper but two or three times a week I did. Sometimes I managed to turn it around and stop my temper by having a sort of crazy conversation with myself or with him or by behaving in a totally daft way: singing crazy silly songs, throwing my hat in the air, doing a silly dance or running around the garden or the house. It helped me. It was like a way of letting off a head of steam to stop the kettle exploding. If only I could have been more detached then I wouldn't have found it so hard not to be angry. And on top of that I was becoming totally exhausted. I wished I could have my old Bobby back... but the new Bobby was sometimes very nice. He had fewer inhibitions and at best he had a childlike gentleness. At worst he would suddenly switch to being an angry, grumpy and swearing old man who looked so bleak it made my heart bleed.

But despite everything I made sure we did a few nice things. I wrote in my diary:

"On Monday we drove to Llandudno and booked into the same B & B as before. Then we had a wander around the town and down to the end of the pier. From there we had a magnificent view of the whole bay: the Great Orme and the Little Orme, all the grand sweep of Victorian hotels and guest houses and of course Venue Cymru where we went that evening to the opera 'La Boheme'. I think it is my favourite opera and was very well done, though the principal tenor's voice was a bit 'plummy'. Bob tried to explain to me in his words of very few syllables what the singer should do to improve it. Mimi, the principal female role, had a beautiful voice, and I cried at the end, when she died.

The next day we drove back through the Conwy valley and onto the A5 at Betws-y-Coed and through the mountains. We stopped to look at the Swallow Falls which are amazing after all the rain we've had recently.

I feel as if I must treasure each good day, each happy moment, for I don't know whether he will be living with me for very much longer. Treasuring the good times gives me strength to deal with the very difficult ones."

***

We went to see Dawn, the speech therapist, again and although Bob was very taken with her I didn't hold out much hope that she could improve his ability to speak. However, she gave me a booklet full of very helpful advice. From the instructions in the booklet I wrote the following poem using almost the exact words that Bob and I spoke on a particular day, an average morning. It did help me to see the funny side of things even though it was getting harder and harder as my dear man's condition worsened.

Language breakdown

(Advice to carers of persons with comprehension and memory problems.)

Repeat messages frequently.

Here are your teeth. You need to put your teeth in.
Here are your teeth.
You need to put them in.
Here are your teeth.

Use short sentences.
They need a scrub first.

Use simple words.
That's right – they're clean now.
Now you can put them in your mouth.
I can't.
Yes you can, they're clean now.
No.
Well you can't eat breakfast without your teeth.

Ask one question at a time.
Do you want your breakfast?
Yes please.
Well you need to put your teeth in first.
No I don't.
Would like a cup of tea or coffee?
Yes please.
Oh Christ!
What's the matter now?
It's this thing!
Do you mean your hair?
No!

Break down instructions into separate components.
Here's your comb.
Thank you.
Now you need to comb your hair.
Yes I know that!

Use a calm, pleasant tone of voice.
There you are, you look really handsome now.

Speak slowly, face to face.
I'm going down stairs to make your breakfast.
Don't forget to put your teeth in

Avoid sending unintentional emotional messages by your manner of speaking.
Here's your breakfast.
Oh no! You've still not got your teeth in.
You're going again at me - you know I – I forget
Don't get up I'll go and get them...

Here they are.
There's only one of them.
No there's two, top and bottom.
Well shall I - you -wear them - in here?
I think maybe you should.

Then there came a time when both Pete and I were at our wit's end. I wrote:

"The other day Pete was cooking a meal for Bob at his house. They had shared a can of beer together as they often did and Pete then left Bob watching the television in the sitting room while he carried on cooking a meal. When he returned Bob had gone. Pete didn't worry too much as Bob had often gone down the road for a short walk in the past and it had only been a matter of walking down the road to find him. This time, however, Pete couldn't find him anywhere. He tried phoning me but I had no signal so he phoned the police. It turned out that Bob had got on a bus to Bangor and then got a bus to Bethesda. The bus driver was worried because Bob apparently told him he was going up the mountains.

He had no coat, let alone a rucksack and was obviously not thinking straight. The bus driver phoned the police and Bob was brought back 'kicking and screaming' – well very angry anyway. It came out in the police report that Pete and Bob had been 'drinking'! Bob's social worker and Social Services then rapped Pete's knuckles and I had to step in and tell them that I was very happy with the care work that Pete did for me and that as far as I was concerned I didn't mind them sharing a beer. Well, I hadn't read the rules! So I had my knuckles rapped too! "

***

Here is the report I gave to social services about this matter:

Report for Social Services re Police report into Peter Cooper drinking while in charge of Robert Treves   29/10/08

1.   I firstly want to point out that I have been very happy with the care that Peter Cooper has provided for Bob and Bob sees Peter as a good friend.

2.   I want to point out that in the summer Peter asked me if it would be alright if he and Bob had the occasional drink together,

and I had given my permission, as long as it was only a small quantity. I never thought that this was against the regulations and so if anyone is to blame it is me, and on the particular evening in question they had shared a can of lager, that was all.

3.   I also want to point out that Bob has a habit of wandering off. He has done it to me as well as with Peter. He does not get lost even though he is classed as a vulnerable adult.

4.   Peter phoned the police partly because I had said that we ought to report such incidences, for the record, so to speak.

5.   Peter and I are now aware that Peter should not drink while he is looking after Bob and he will therefore not do so in future.

**

After this sort of 'support' both Pete and I felt we needed a break. I pointed out to Angharad that Social Services seemed more concerned about a tiny social drink than the fact that Bob had gone missing and if it had not been for the sensible bus driver he might have been wandering around the Carneddau mountains. This wasn't the first time he had disappeared from home. He was always wandering away from home and really I had no way of stopping him nor did I want to. I knew how vital freedom to roam was to Bob. He never seemed to get lost and always came home sooner or later.

Often friends and neighbours would meet him and suggest he went home and generally he would. Because of this persistent wandering I had asked the police about a month before if they could inform bus drivers not to let him on the buses. It definitely worked. I remember one day after this he came home very angry.

"The bus driver wouldn't let me get on!" but with this trip to Bethesda he obviously encountered bus drivers who didn't know him.

**

On top of everything else, Kira phoned me. She sounded on the point of having a break down, sobbing down the phone, "Please Mum, I need your help!" So I arranged for Bob to go into the 'awful home' while I went down to Cornwall to look after my grandchildren for a few days. (There weren't any vacancies in any other homes, so it had to be that one). Perhaps I should have wondered why? I wrote in my diary:

"Tomorrow my Bobby goes to the 'awful' home again. I tried to find a different residential home but none could have him at such short notice. Pete needs a break from Bob and so do I. I know social services are giving me the maximum amount of time allowed for his care which is thirty two hours a week. It sounds a lot but there are one hundred and sixty eight hours in a week. If Bob had anything like a normal dementia thirty two hours might be fine... maybe... but Bob seems to have untold energy to wake up, get up half the night and create havoc all day long. It's a bit like having a two year old with ADHD in a big, very strong man's body. These last few days, when he's having a temper tantrum I have to jump clear of his arms and legs in case I get knocked flying. I know he has no intention of hurting me. He's just angry and unaware that I am there. It's more than a bit scary. So far this has only happened a couple of times. Hopefully it won't happen that often.

I told Bob this morning that he will be going to the home tomorrow but I haven't reminded him tonight... tomorrow will be soon enough. If I tell him now he probably will refuse to go. It's only for two weeks and then we can get back to looking after him, feeling refreshed.

It's been a hectic day. I've sold our campervan Charlie for £2200. I'm sad, as we have had some good times in the van. But Bob has been refusing to ride in it ever since I hurt my arm driving all over the mountains with his friend Jan. I still have the little car but it suddenly conked out and is now at the garage. Holger has lent me his car to get to the home tomorrow and another friend is taking me to the station to catch the train to Penzance on Sunday."

So Bob went to the residential home. I couldn't sleep the night before. I was so tense and worried that he would refuse to go. I was feeling guilty about him going anyway and worried that I wouldn't be at home if it really was that awful. I wouldn't be nearby. I packed the car with his things the night before and once we were on our way I explained, once again, where we were going and why and that it would only be for a short while... a little less than two weeks. When we got to the home he was very intent on the fact that he needed to have a pee, so while he rushed into the bushes I got all his stuff to the front door and a member of staff took it in.

When Bob emerged from the bushes it was just a matter of getting him inside. He then began to realise where he was. We walked along the corridor to his room at the far end. I could feel Bob getting agitated. It was not a very nice room. It was very cramped and it smelt musty. A lick of paint would have cheered it up. In fact the whole home looked as though it needed decorating but all the members of staff seem caring. Bob got more and more angry. He wouldn't say goodbye... he spoke very clearly.

"I don't know how you can do this to me!"

"But Bobby, I have to go to Cornwall and you have to have someone to look after you."

"I can look after myself!"

"No you can't anymore."

"Yes I can."

I left quickly, and stood outside the home trying to fight back the tears and thinking to myself, "Dear Bobby... I wish... I wish you could look after yourself but you are like a snowman gradually melting. The old Bobby has lost his features... his arms are drooping... his knees are bending... his face is gradually disappearing before my eyes. My darling love, I know that when I meet you in heaven you will be restored and perfect... but there is nothing that can be done in this life but accept..." and with that I drove back across Anglesey.

***

The next day I caught the early train to Cornwall. It seemed that everyone was ill with flu, everyone that was except the children. I spent a few very busy days looking after them until Kira was back on her feet. At least I got several good nights' sleep! About a week later, I caught the train home again.

Once I was home I rang to see how Bob was. The woman I spoke to seemed to be very fussed about the fact that he wouldn't go in the shower and that he wouldn't wear pyjamas. I tried to explain that he never had a shower at home. He liked to either have a strip wash or a bath and he never wore pyjamas. I should have told them not to fuss about these things. Surely other things were more important. I felt really upset so I went down to the residential home with a heavy heart.

The manager of the home reported that he'd been an extremely "naughty boy", whatever that was supposed to mean. They didn't seem keen to give any details but I gathered he wouldn't be welcome there again. He seemed worse and a bit confused. Poor Bobby, he was glad to climb into his own bed and had a long sleep the first night back.

In the second half of November I bought a blue VW Polo with the money I'd had from selling Charlie the campervan. She was a lovely car. I now needed to sell the little Aixam car but I couldn't seem to find a buyer. Also I kept feeling ill. Bob was not sleeping and I really felt I needed someone to come and be with him two or three nights a week so I could get some sleep. I wondered how much longer I could go on.

Since he'd returned from the home, his temper was far worse, usually because of problems getting dressed. He frequently would become like a whirling dervish, waving arms and legs around with hopeless violent anger at his inability to make any sense of socks and trousers and shirts. I would have to jump out of the way or be flattened. It wasn't happening every day, but much more frequently than before, and often enough to make me feel jumpy. When he got into this sort of state he wasn't aware of his surroundings so sometimes he'd crash into things. One day my favourite fruit bowl was broken when he crashed into the Welsh dresser and the plates fell off onto the fruit bowl. Another day my favourite mug was broken in a similar way and yet another day he tore the seam of his trousers when he tried to put both his feet into one trouser leg. I constantly felt like a piece of chewed string and my whole body ached with tension and tiredness. But when he was calm and happy he would sing to me and hold me in his arms just as he had always done.

I wrote in my diary:

"If only I could get some sleep. I don't want to let Bobby go again. I don't want to give up on him. I know my strength is ebbing away. I know I will have to give up soon but I don't want to. A big part of me still clings to his loving being, warm and wholesome, despite this wretched disease which is eating his thinking, his speech, his logic and his identity."

***

At the end of November I found someone who could come and stay overnight two or three nights a week. I was going to pay for her out of my own money as Social Services couldn't give me any more financial help. She seemed nice but Bob refused to have her.

"I'm not having some strange woman here!"

"But Bobby, I need to be able to sleep. If I can't get enough sleep then I can't look after you anymore my love."

"I don't need looking after!"

"Please Bobby."

"No!"

So we went to the doctor's and he gave me some liquid sleeping stuff that was a bit stronger than the sleeping tablets. I also tried giving him an extra seroquel tablet but nothing made much difference. I thought that perhaps I could try an herbal remedy, sunervin, if he'd take it. I couldn't put all his medicine in one honey sandwich! Meanwhile, the doctor examined me and said he thought I might be developing a stomach ulcer. I told the doctor I thought it was just that I was exhausted. With Bob refusing to have anyone to sleep over I was not sure I could carry on much longer. I tried again and again to explain this to Bob, but he insisted he didn't want some stranger staying the night. I couldn't ask Pete to do anymore hours and anyway Bob was not keen on Pete staying overnight, though he had done so several times. Part of me clung on, wanting to keep him with me and another part of me, the exhausted part, just wanted to let go of this hard responsibility.

Friends said that I shouldn't feel bad about letting Bob go into a home and that they didn't know how I could keep going.

**

One Sunday I took Bob to Bangor Quaker meeting. Everyone was delighted to see us and Bob behaved really well and enjoyed the fuss they made of him and the tea and biscuits. I went home thinking to myself that if only Bob could behave well every day I could cope, but the good days were becoming less frequent.

At the end of November I had a day and a night's break – I went to Gillian's second 'Earth Walking' weekend. Pete came to stay but Bob didn't want me to go. Pete just said, "Go!" so I did. The course was wonderful though every time we did any sort of meditation, I just fell asleep! But it was so good just to have a night and a day away from Bob. More and more I could never relax when I was at home. If I left him for more than a few minutes he often ended up doing something dangerous, like turning the gas on or pouring water all over an electric heater. He would constantly break things or lose things. One day I found half my plant pots had disappeared. He'd carried them up to the top of the garden and thrown them into the bushes. Years later, long after he had gone I was still finding smaller things in the garden; a pair of his glasses under a rose bush, knives and forks and spoons hidden under rocks and bushes.

At the beginning of December we went to the Memory Clinic and the doctor increased Bob's medication. Angharad, Bob's social worker, was there and said that she thought it was time that Bob went into a nursing home permanently. I did tell her that he would sometimes flail his arms and legs all over the place when he was in a temper, wildly breaking things or tearing things in the process and that this was happening a lot more frequently.

"I suppose I am in danger of being flattened though I know Bob would never intentionally hurt me", I said. At this Angharad said that it was definitely time he went into a home.

"I can't make such a decision, though I don't know if I can take much more", was all I would say.

It was another day, a beautiful day. Bob had gone off with Pete, reluctantly, and I was in heaven, sitting on a rock half way up Cwm Silyn. It was a bright cold day and there were little pockets of snow all around me but Snowdon was well covered. The sun was shining and the air was still, but over the sea dark clouds were building and there was more snow and wind in the forecast. I could hear a dog barking in the distance. It was time to go home and get in before it went dark. I had a short story to write for my M.A. I sat still, a few minutes longer, feeling a slight breeze in my hair. I got out my diary and started to write a poem:

In dreams I walk in a forever time

where there is no ending,

and no heart breaking,

just each day, a new beginning.

And then I walked home and continued to stagger through nights and days where time was not on my side.

***

On December 14th the decision was taken out of my hands and by then I was far too ill to protest. Bob was to go into the dementia ward at the hospital for assessment and then on to somewhere, a nursing home with a secure unit, permanently. I remember gathering a few changes of clothing for him and putting them into a bag with his washing and shaving gear. I remember thinking – "Oh dear, he still has no pyjamas... maybe they won't mind in the hospital, maybe they'll give him some..."

I remember everything seemed to be in a thick fog of suffering. My head thundered. It felt about to split open. Pete drove us there.

I was so ill I could hardly stand up but somehow I walked along the corridors to the dementia ward. I remember the door was locked and we had to press a button. A nurse opened the door. I remember filling in forms and telling the nurse that Bob had to have his medicine in a honey sandwich. I remember all this as if it was happening on the other side of a thick plate glass door.

It wasn't really happening to me. It wasn't really happening to Bob. And then I was trying to say goodbye but Bob was wandering around and ignored me.

Pete drove me home. He made me a cup of tea and a hot water bottle and left. I remember that the sheets felt cool against my thumping head and then I slept.

Chapter 9

Letting Go

You have been my soul's growth.
So now you' re gone
I'll not let you be my soul's loss,
nor look at you with sorrow.
With all my strength
I will go on.

I wrote in my diary:

"*Bob is now in the Dementia Unit at Bangor hospital. He went in on Tuesday. Pete drove us in. I was so ill I could barely stand. I was burning up with a temperature. There were forms to fill in, details of his care to give, goodbyes to say. Then Pete took me home and I have hardly risen from my bed since then. A friend has popped in a couple of times with food that I cannot eat. I have crawled out of bed for a drink of water and a pee and then I have slept and slept and slept. Gillian and Holger would have called but they are ill with the flu too and so are Deb and Andy. Today, four days later, is the first day I have sat up in bed and written and read a little. I'm reading a wonderful book that Gillian lent me. I need to lie down again now. Maybe I'll read a bit more and then sleep some more.*"

The next day I felt a lot better. I rang the hospital. I asked how Bob was but they weren't very forthcoming. I gathered they were finding him difficult. I explained that I still felt too ill to drive in to see him but that I would do so as soon as I was well enough. I didn't want to ask Pete to help. He was also exhausted by Bob and deserved a rest and a peaceful Christmas.

***

Two days later I went into see Bob. It had been a week since we had left him in the dementia ward but I was still very weak and shaky on my feet. I was so upset and angry at what I found.

I found a man who looked like a shrunken tramp, all bent over. I had been ill for a week and in all that time he was still wearing the same clothes he came in. His trousers were filthy. He had a seven day growth of beard and a great big bruise on his hand where he had been hitting the door. The nurses told me he'd been trying to escape.

Nobody seemed to really care. I took him into his room with the intention of helping him wash and shave and help him into some clean clothes. But I couldn't find his shaving bag or his wash bag and all his socks seem to have disappeared apart from the ones he'd got on. I asked the nurses if they knew what had happened to his things but they seemed to be too busy filling in forms to be of any help and would only say that he wasn't allowed to keep razors for health and safety reasons.

So I left the ward and went down to the WRVS shop to get some extra supplies of things he needed. I came back and helped him shave and wash and get into clean clothes. Then I stayed to talk to him, but he just went and lay down on his bed. I kissed him and gave his poor tense shoulders a massage. He looked thinner so I don't think he can have eaten much this last few days.   I gave him the grapes I'd brought in for him and his favourite Snickers bar. He munched them slowly and then lay down again.

"I love you," I said.

"And I love you too."

And with that he went to sleep.

I left his room, holding back the tears. I asked to see the nurse in charge and was shown to her office.

"Can I help you?" she said.

"Yes. Why has Bob been left in such a terrible state? I have been ill or I would have come in sooner, but in the seven days since he arrived it doesn't look as if anyone has helped him wash or shave or put clean clothes on."

"Whenever anyone tried to help him he waved them away. It's our policy in this ward, in these circumstances to leave the person alone."

"But this is a dementia ward. Surely your nurses must be trained to deal with difficult cases like Bob."

"Well he is very difficult and that is our policy."

"What about his medication? Has he been taking it?"

"No, he won't take it."

"Well I left instructions that he should be given it in a honey or jam sandwich."

"We can't do that without the consultant's permission."

"But the consultant knew that he wouldn't take his medication any other way and had already given me his permission. I told the lady who was filling in his form a week ago about this. It should be down on his notes. No wonder he's been so difficult. He's probably been having hallucinations again, poor man."

"Well, we are going to start him on a new medication. It can be given with patches."

I didn't know what else to say to the woman but as I left she told me, rather as if it was my fault, that Bob had got into her office during the week and damaged two of the computers. I felt like saying once again that this was a dementia ward for goodness sake! Dementia patients will break things.

I instead said. "Well, maybe you should keep your office locked at all times."

I could have laughed except that I was close to tears. Some bloody awful dementia ward!

***

Just before Christmas Angharad, Bob's social worker, and I had a meeting with Dr Kissane, another consultant. He was tall and young with spiked hair and had one eye that wandered sideways. It was a bit disconcerting and I wondered if he was blind in that eye. Anyway he came across as a good and caring man who seemed to understand how torn I was at giving up on Bob.

"Our backs are against the wall," he said, "There is no more money for extra care for Bob if he stays at home."

I knew there wasn't.

"And so he's going to have to go into a care home and a specialist one at that as he will need to be in a secure unit with staff that have specialist training in how to deal with his violent tendencies."

There were other people at the meeting and they told me that there were three possible care homes within reasonable travelling distance that had units for persons classed as being EMI.

"What does that stand for?" I asked.

"Elderly Mentally Infirm."

I felt a bit shaken that he had been put in a box labelled "Elderly Mentally Infirm," and that he was to be locked into a building, a secure unit, for the rest of his life. I found it hard to accept that this was how he was now seen by the authorities. It felt as if he was being punished for his illness but there was nothing I could do but accept the situation and make the best of it.

Christmas came and went and every day I drove to Bangor hospital to visit Bob. I made a conscious decision not to be angry with what I regarded, at first, as the incompetence of the staff in the dementia ward. I realised that it wasn't their fault that most of their time seemed to be taken up with filling in forms. Also looking around at the other people who were patients I realised that Bob could appear to the nurses to be the most frightening person there. So every day I did what I could to help them and to show them how to look after him. He seemed a lot happier now that I was visiting every day. I also decided to go and see two of the three homes. One had a long waiting list so although it came highly recommended, I didn't bother to visit that one. He needed to be settled somewhere as soon as possible and I could always put his name down on their waiting list if the one I chose was no good.

In the end I decided on the nearest one. It would be easy for me to visit as it was only a ten minute drive away and was in a lovely setting with trees and nature all around. The rooms were nice and there was a feeling of spaciousness. The other home was by a main road and just didn't feel right for Bob. I hoped I had made the right decision.

***

I had also been worrying about money. How would I manage financially without Bob? I would no longer have his rent or his share of the cost of the household bills which were quite big because it was a big house. I had a little money from a couple of investments plus my state pension but that was not enough to cover the bills. When he went into care permanently all his allowances and state pension would go towards paying for his care in a Care Home. I still hadn't been able to sell the little car. Nobody in this area seemed to want such an unusual car especially as it had lots of things wrong with it. In the end Kira and Angel said they would buy it off me. It was not worth much anyway but the extra money would be a great help. So I drove it down to Cornwall. It broke down twice on the way! I spent New Year with them and found a cheap train ticket to take me home.

On New Years' Eve I wrote:

"I've read Amber and Jasper a story but Rosy has already gone to bed. Now peace reigns. They are all asleep. Kira and Angel are at a New Year's party and I shall probably be asleep long before midnight. I'm still far from well after that bout of flu. Perhaps I should make some New Year's resolutions but I'm a bit tired just now.

I have contacted the nearest home, Plas y Bryn, to confirm that I want Bob to go there.

What will this New Year bring now that Bob will not be living with me anymore? I feel such a mixture of deep sadness and guilt that I couldn't carry on, but also hope that he will be happy enough in the home. I also feel relief that this heavy burden of responsibility will be lifted from me."

***

I got back home late on New Year's Day and went straight around to the hospital the next day. Bob looked awful. He had lost so much weight and once again was sitting in a corner hunched up, unkempt and unshaven. No one seemed to care. They just said he was difficult. I felt like putting in an official complaint but I didn't have the energy to do it. I felt totally *underwhelmed* by the Dementia Ward's 'care'. Once again I helped him to get shaved and washed and then I got out a little CD player and some CDs I'd brought with me as a present for him. We played the CDs and Bob sang a little. I thought to myself. "They say that their policy is to leave him alone when he's difficult, when what he needs is loving and caring attention. Oh my poor dear man. Part of me feels now that I should never have given up, but I know logically that I couldn't cope anymore."

On the 8th January, Bob left the hospital and went to live at the nursing home, Plas y Bryn. Pete and I went over to the hospital to pick him up and take him there. I just had to trust that they would look after him with a lot more care than the dementia unit.

Time went by and Bob seemed reasonably settled at the home. He had a new friend named Betty who snuggled up to him and looked at him with adoring eyes. She seemed to think that I was his mother! I think this confused him a bit so sometimes he called me 'Mother' instead of Ali.

He sometimes had accidents.

One day I found he'd peed into his CD player so it didn't work anymore. Another time I found he'd broken the window, another time the door handle to his room was ripped off. I bought him another CD player but he peed into that as well so I decided I wouldn't be leaving anymore CD players in his room. Perhaps he thought they were potties!

"He doesn't always sleep", the staff told me – don't I know it – "And then he gets confused and things get broken". Most of the staff were very patient and kind.

Dr Kissane came to visit him. He asked him lots of questions and each time Bob's reply was just gobbledygook – his ability to speak had got so much worse – but then he asked

"Are you happy here?" and Bob immediately and emphatically replied "Oh yes!"

***

I generally visited about three or more times a week and after the first couple of weeks or so I asked them if I might take him out and they said that I could. So the first time we went for a drive to Dinas Dinlle and walked a little by the sea. The next time we went to Aberdesach and began to walk along beside the chalets. Bob suddenly stopped and pulled his trousers down and crouched down by the track and did a poo right there. There was nothing I could do to stop him and luckily no one was close by. I had some tissues in my bag and I offered them to him to wipe himself.

It felt very odd, this total lack of inhibition, like a small child. "My dear man", I thought, "what has become of you?" I knew I had to try and accept that he would go on and on, getting worse. From then on, when I took him out, I always asked him if he needed to go to the toilet before we went off for a walk!

It was the beginning of February and I took Bob to visit Gillian and Holger. They made a great fuss of him while he enjoyed munching Gillian's delicious cakes. Holger was late back as he'd decided to walk to work as there was still a lot of snow on the road further up the Nantlle valley. Meanwhile, I trimmed Gillian's dad's and Bob's toenails. There were times when Bob would look so vacant, although he always seemed to recognise me. Sometimes I felt he had drifted away entirely from the man he had been, but on this day at Gillian's he seemed much better and happily chatted away to us all. Mostly it was all nonsense to us but we nodded and smiled and it obviously made sense to him. I preferred to pretend that I could understand what he was saying. Often I could make an educated guess. It was also difficult to be sure how much he understood us. If I kept the things I said quite simple, it seemed to help him and he would often give a short answer in comprehensible words. Then it was fairly obvious that he had understood.

Music was our best form of communication now. Whenever we were driving somewhere I played some of his favourite music: sometimes opera, sometimes folk songs, sometimes classical music. He particularly loved Bryn Terfel's CD 'We'll Keep a Welcome'.

When I took him back to the home after our outing to Gillian's, I was told that Dawn, his speech therapist, was coming to see him the following Wednesday so I made a mental note to be there.

However on the Wednesday Dawn rang me. "Where are you?" she asked.

I had completely forgotten it was Wednesday. I apologised profusely. She said that Bob's speech was much worse and that she didn't feel there was anything more she could do. I said I quite understood and that yes, he was getting worse and I thanked her very much for all her kindness and help. She just said that she wished me and Bob well and that was that. I decided to drop a card into the speech therapy centre to thank her. She had been so kind to us both.

***

The days stretched out and I felt sometimes that I was going slightly crazy, forgetting the time, forgetting the day. I hoped I wasn't getting dementia too... I dreamt and remembered my dreams and I wrote a lot too. The snow had fallen a few days before but was now gradually receding. Sometimes I walked Jazz, the dog, for Andy and Deb and sometimes I just walked. I missed the old Bob so much; it was like an unfillable hole in my heart. I would wake from dreaming that he was lying beside me, all warm and cuddly. Then I'd remember he would never sleep beside me again. I missed our love making. I could still hug him and kiss him when I saw him and that was a comfort but sometimes he hugged and kissed the women in the home too. I knew it was just the dementia. I knew that the dementia caused him to lose his inhibitions but it sometimes felt a bit embarrassing... but in a way it didn't seem to upset the women. It was not done with any sexual intent. In fact it was as though he had become like a little boy again, in need of a childish kiss or a hug.

**

On February 10th I brought Bob home for the first time since he'd left, almost two months ago. I was worried that if I brought him home too soon he might refuse to go back to the nursing home. So, still worried about this possibility, I arranged with Andy and Deb that after visiting our house we would go for a walk and then go to their place for a cup of coffee and then leave their place and not ours to go back to Plas y Bryn.

In the end I really had nothing to worry about. Bob was delighted to be home and to have his favourite leek and potato soup for lunch. In his own way, he tried to say that although it was lovely to visit, he knew I couldn't look after him anymore.

We wandered around and up the lane and then back to Andy and Deb's for coffee. Afterwards Andy said he could see how much his speech had deteriorated but that he seemed more content, happy even. I think generally he was. The home was a safe place for him and they were genuinely kind and caring there. I was so glad I'd got over this hurdle and from then on I brought him back home fairly often.

A week or so later I wrote:

"I took Bob home again today. We had just had a cup of tea when he started to give signs that he needed the loo. I went upstairs with him but we didn't get there soon enough and he had wet himself slightly. I helped him get into dry clothes and then we took Jazz for a walk. He loves Jazz and enjoyed the walk but he was exhausted afterwards. His legs have become much thinner and he has become more wobbly when he's walking on rough ground.

I noticed the other day at the care home that he was wearing a nappy. I told the carers that he didn't need one but perhaps I was wrong and perhaps soon he will have to wear one all the time. It feels like a very final indignity but I suppose it's better than having accidents in your pants. The old Bob would have loathed such an indignity but my dear man is floating away from who he was."

***

Sometimes I would just visit Bob and not take him out at all. Maybe the weather was foul or there were other problems. Sometimes we would just sit in his room and I would bring the CD player in and we'd play some music. One day when I arrived I couldn't understand what Bob was doing. He kept sticking his tongue out. I then remembered that he liked to scrub his tongue with a toothbrush so we went along to his little bathroom but I couldn't find any toothbrushes. I realised he'd lost his teeth too.

I searched high and low and then found he'd got the bottom set tightly held in his hand. The staff at the home looked around for his top set and we found some that I thought might be his.

Anyway he seemed happy with them. Then we finally set off to see Frieda and Ray but we didn't stay very long. Frieda just wanted to talk to me and I wanted to include Bob in the conversation. We went back home and had lunch. I'd already cooked a chicken risotto so I was glad he had his teeth in!

When we got back to the Plas y Bryn I told the boss about Bob's teeth and he told me a funny story about when he first worked as a carer. There was an old lady, very petite sitting next to a large man, eating. They both took their teeth out and then swapped them. The old woman looked like Goofy and the old man nearly lost hers in his big mouth. The staff had an awful job persuading them to swap back.

A few days later the staff in Bob's section told me that they'd found out that one of the residents liked stealing false teeth so that was why Bob's teeth had been going missing. Also Bob's 'girlfriend', Betty, was beginning to get on Bob's nerves. She never left his side and it was making him grumpy. The staff decided it would be best to move her to one of the other sections. I hoped Bob wouldn't be upset by this but I think in the end he was quite glad she'd gone.

One night when I couldn't sleep with all these thoughts pointlessly churning around in my head, I sat up in bed and wrote this poem.

Wish Bone

There's a wishbone sitting on the worktop,

dried up, waiting to be pulled,

but no one to pull it with.

No one to come home to, to say -

'Look at these lovely shells I collected,'

to smile and say 'umm'.

There is just the cat

and she can't pull the wishbone

or wish that this did not have to happen.

We were supposed to grow old touching,

making tea, listening to our favourite songs

and sharing the light in each other's eyes.

But your light went out.

The dried-up dumb blank grew

and you were gone before you went

to that other Home where I visit

and you give a vacant worried smile

and call me – 'Mother.'

I did worry sometimes. Was I hanging onto Bob too much? Was I taking him out too much or not enough? Had I failed him by not keeping him at home?

I submitted "Wish Bone," to a poetry magazine on the advice of my M.A. tutor and I also read it, along with a few other poems, at a poetry evening in Bangor. Several friends said it moved them to tears and how could I read it and not cry? All I could say was that I had done so much crying in the privacy of my own home that there were no more tears left in me.

I missed the old Bob so much but I kept myself busy and that helped me to remain positive. I'd joined an indoor bowling club. I was pretty useless at bowling but the people were friendly. I sometimes went to quiz night at the local pub. I was pretty useless at that too! Then there was my M.A. course every Tuesday evening which I really enjoyed. I had made some good friends there and I thought my writing was improving. Then there was the Welsh class and I also went to a yoga class.

I enjoyed walking and working in my garden and chatting to the neighbours and I kept smiling. But I had times when I felt so lonely and so sad. I looked back and berated myself for the way I had behaved towards Bob, getting angry with him for his behaviour when he couldn't help how he behaved. The thoughts went around and around in my head: maybe I should have tried harder. I could have been more patient etc. etc. I wished I could have looked after Bob right to the end of his life but at least I went to see him every other day.

It was March and I wasn't sleeping well. I thought about going away so I could see things in a fresh light. Several friends had offered to help me tidy up Bob's stuff. They said, "You don't need to go away. You just need to clear the house. And don't go to see him so much". Well, I knew they meant well but I wanted to see Bob whenever I could and I was not ready to clear his things away. He came back home regularly and I wanted him to feel this was still his home. If his things had gone I'd feel like a traitor even though he might not miss them.

***

During the spring and summer of 2009, Bob's condition became fairly stable. Dr Kissane had explained to me that with Bob's type of dementia there would periods of relative stability and periods when the condition would go into freefall. He did gradually become more incontinent and a bit more wobbly on his legs and his speech continued to slowly deteriorate. Most of his words would be a bit like funny sounds and I would just do my best to guess what he was trying to say. I took him out whenever I could but we generally went to places where he could walk on the flat. Occasionally I took him to an afternoon concert at the local theatre but more often we would come back to the house or visit friends.

One memorable day we went to Dinas Dintlle to visit Frieda and Ray. It was a beautiful afternoon so we took Ray out in his wheelchair. There was a road and then a concrete path all the way to the café. Bob was very enthusiastic about pushing Ray in his wheelchair and Frieda and I had to gently restrain and guide him otherwise Ray might have ended up being tipped out onto the beach! He was always so good natured and just giggled when Bob went a bit fast. He liked the speed but Frieda didn't and despite the dementia Bob was still very strong. When we got to the other end we all had ice creams and sat on a bench in the sun for a while.

On the way back Bob was tired and content to let Frieda and I push Ray most of the way. There were a few families on the beach; children and adults making sandcastles. I pointed to them and Bob tried to say something. I guessed he was saying that he remembered making sandcastles with Amber and Jasper and Rosy. I spoke about this and I could see by the way his face lit up that I had understood correctly. By the time we got back to Frieda's both Ray and Bob were tired so I said goodbye and we drove back to Plas y Bryn listening to some of his favourite music on the way.

***

When the weather was foul or he was too tired to go out, we would sit in his room or in the lounge and listen to music. I always kept a CD player in my car and not in his room after the peeing episodes. I also regularly took to staying for a meal at the home. My presence would help and encourage Bob to sit down to eat.

He was becoming more and more inclined to wander up and down the corridor with his plate and fork, spilling bits of food as he went. Also his eating wasn't helped by the fact that he kept losing his teeth. Once or twice I actually caught the resident 'false teeth thief' red handed as he snatched some false teeth off one or other of the residents when they had taken their teeth out for some reason or other. He would then make off at great speed for one old man. On several occasions I followed him to watch what he might do with the teeth. Sometimes he would try to put them in his own mouth or in his pocket but I also saw him trying to hide the teeth by dropping them in a bin or down the back of a radiator.

There were also times when Bob lost his shoes or his slippers or other things. Most of the residents in Bob's section had no understanding as to what was theirs and what was someone else's, so it was not unusual to see an old man making off in a pair of lady's slippers or vice versa. Most of the staff were wonderfully kind and patient and did their best to restore belongings to the right people in the midst of all their other caring responsibilities.

***

With Bob seemingly settled, I was able to spend more of the spring and summer with my family. I went to Cornwall a couple of times. Also Alexis came to stay in the early summer and Kira and the granddaughters came up to me in early August.

I remember one day soon after Kira, Rosy and Amber arrived to stay with me, I told Kira I was going to take Bob out for the day. She was very nervous. She hadn't seen him in a while. I had told her how thin he now was but still fairly fit. I had told her he could be difficult though very rarely with me and that he couldn't speak much now except gobbledygook. "Well, I'd like to see him but perhaps only for a short while as I want to take the girls to a thing called 'The Wild Child'. It's going to be lots of fun for them."

Anyway I went to fetch Bob. The girls said could they come too but their mum said no. She really was nervous. I told Bob that he was going to see Amber and Rosy and Kira and he obviously understood and made all sorts of excited sounds.

When we got home, Amber and Rosy were sitting at my big kitchen table painting pictures. Kira gave him a little hug and then Bob sat down with the girls grinning from ear to ear.

"Hello Bobby, would you like to paint too?"

"Hello," he managed, and then "Yes."

He then tried to say more but it was all jumbled sounds. The girls giggled and he giggled too.

"Would you like something to eat?" Kira was making some salad. She gave him some and a fork to eat it with. This was all too confusing for Bob. He tried to eat the salad with his paintbrush and paint with the fork. Amber and Rosy laughed, he laughed and soon we were all giggling our heads off. Kira said quietly to me.

"He's just like a big kid. I don't know why I was so worried."

Later we played some music and Bob started to dance. Amber got up and danced with him and then we all danced.

Kira was packing a picnic.

"Can Bobby come too?"

"Of course he can."

So I rang Plas Y Bryn to say Bob would be late back and off we went.

It was in a beautiful valley with tepees and a campfire and a sort of campfire oven that cooked bread and all sorts of delicious things. One tepee had art and craft things for kids. There was music and games and families having fun. After an hour or two we suddenly realised Bob was missing. I had a moment of panic but then Kira spotted him walking away from the campsite at speed.

"I think Bobby's making a bid for freedom", she said.

We ran after him and steered him back with the promise of a cup of tea and more food. Then we all drove back singing and chatting.

I think Bob was very tired by the end and glad to be back at Plas y Bryn, but it was a very special day.

***

After a while I went back to working for myself as a chiropodist and reflexologist. I also bit the bullet over a lot of Bob's stuff. Jenn, Dafydd's girlfriend, came and helped me sort through his hundreds of books and CDs. I kept some of them, but over half went to the charity shop, along with the clothes that no longer fitted him. He had lost so much weight.

In late August, Bob began to be a bit more difficult. One day he grabbed one poor woman by the hand (she was the wife of one of the residents) and dragged her all the way down the corridor. She was very frightened. Bob was still so strong. Another time he got a hold of someone's foot and nearly pulled them off the chair. He was becoming more restless at meal times and even my presence didn't seem to stop him from walking around with his food. He was sleeping badly again too. The nurses at the home told me that they had called Dr Kurian in to see him and he had changed his medication.

One morning soon after this, I walked to Gillian's home for a massage. My car was at the garage being serviced. It was a lovely day and I'd planned to sit in the sun later and string the onions and then go for a walk up the mountains.

After my massage Gillian said "Your bag is making noises".

"That'll be my phone."

It was a message from Bob's care home to say that Bob had collapsed and was at the hospital. Of course, sod's law, I had no car. Gillian thought of ringing Holger, but I rang the home back and they, very kindly, came and picked me up. When I got to the hospital one of Bob's carers, a lovely girl, was by his side in the corridor. They were waiting for a bed in the ward. My phone went again. It was the garage ringing to say that the car was now ready to pick up, so the man from Bob's home kindly took me all the way back to Penygroes. I drove home, grabbed a bite to eat and then went back to the hospital. There I found my dear Bobby in Tryfan Ward snoring away. The lovely carer was still with him. She went to the cafe to get us both a cup of tea.

A few days later Bob was discharged. The doctor thought it might have been the change in his medication that caused him to collapse though A&E thought he'd had a heart attack. The hospital asked me to take a letter to his G.P. and I said I would but a few days later Bob was back in hospital. I wasn't sure why, but this time he was in the dementia ward, the same ward he'd been in before Christmas. I went to see him as soon as I could.

"What do you want!" he said crossly. He then cheered up, realising it was me. We sat by the window and watched the most beautiful sunset. I was told by the head nurse that he had to come back in while his new medication was sorted out. I just had to hope he would settle in there okay and that he'd receive better treatment than last time.

The next afternoon I went to visit Bob again. The nurses complained that he had been very difficult. He had got into their computer room and had started taking the place apart.

"This happened last time he was here", I said. "He is difficult. That's probably why he's here." Then I realised that I'd been a bit sarcastic and felt a bit guilty but surely, should they not have kept the room locked?

I stayed to help Bob feel more settled. I wanted to help him get washed and shaved, but the staff nurse wouldn't let me have a razor to shave him. She said it was because he'd been so difficult. She said she needed to risk assess him having a safety razor even though I would be using it. I thought to myself, "I must not judge or mock. They have their job to do. And I know just how difficult he can be." Later the nurses let us out for a walk around the tiny garden courtyard. It was so dreary. I couldn't help hating the place after what happened to Bob last time he was here. I found out that they would be moving the whole unit to Llangefni.

"Hopefully it will be a better environment for the staff and the patients there" I thought to myself.

***

It was mid-September and Bob was still in the dementia ward. The hospital rang. Bob had had another 'episode' as they called it, but not as bad as before. Again his blood pressure had dropped and he had passed out. He then slept for hours. I went to see him as soon as possible but by then he had woken up. He seemed okay, quite calm and happy to see me and while I was there he had something to eat and drink and then went to sleep again. I sat beside his bed for a while and then drove home.

Next day I went to see him again. He was up, but not dressed or shaved so I helped him to do these things and to have something to eat. He was so very tired and wobbly and afterwards all he wanted to do was lie down again. I went home very worried that he might be going to die soon. I lay awake that night thinking that I must prepare myself for this and also sort out his funeral.

Before Bob had become so ill we had talked about having a 'green' burial: we had both liked that idea. I had planned on buying a joint plot for us both in the Green Burial Woodland on the Llyn Peninsula, the Eternal Forest, but as yet I had done nothing about it. I lay awake worrying that I wasn't prepared in any way. I just had not faced up to the fact that Bob could die and now it seemed it could be sooner rather than later. I knew I had to face up to it but I didn't want to. "Not just now" I thought to myself. I wrote this poem and then I tried to sleep.

Worry buried under a blanket

Fear and pain are well covered with a blanket,
keeping them warm for another day,
when I can face them.

Just not now.

Awareness dulled by comforters:
food, drink, and the constant drivel
of the television.
Drugged, boozed oblivion
to blanket it even thicker.

Face it tomorrow.

Bob dancing with Amber

Chapter 10

Running Down Hill

It was September 25th 2009. The doctors and nurses were discussing Bob's medication. They had asked me to sit in on the meeting. I didn't really understand why. In the end, they seemed to be arguing over matters I really didn't understand so I excused myself and left them to it.

I went for a swim in Bangor swimming pool and tried to wash away all my fears and frustrations. The only thing I wanted was for Bob to be able to go back to Plas y Bryn where I could visit him easily and where he was well cared for, but there was some 'problem' which no one seemed willing or able to explain to me that meant he couldn't go back for the time being.

Later on, I went back to the ward with some cakes. I found out that Bob had been in an agitated state. The nurses had given him something to help him calm down. He was now walking up and down, pushing an empty wheelchair and singing to one of the nurses. I took his hand and we went and sat down. I shared some of the cake with him and gave some to the other patients and nurses. Then we went to his room and I snuggled up next to him and played his favourite music. For a moment, I wished we could climb into bed and make passionate love. Memories of desire washed through me and I had to take a strong hold of myself. There was no point in wishing he could be as he *used to be*. I left the CD player with him as he wanted to carry on listening to John McCormack and Di Stefano. I left him singing along to the music and went home for my tea.

When I arrived home, I met one of my neighbours whose well-meant over sympathetic words had me almost in tears. Sometimes I felt so sad and overwhelmed by this hospital situation.

The next day I wrote in my diary:

"My dear Bobby, you've done it again! Oh no! I got to the hospital and found he'd peed in his CD player. That's the third or fourth one he's wrecked. Oh well, at least it was only a cheap one. I called into the care home on the way back as one of the staff had some windfall apples for me. They told me there's every chance Bob will be able to come back next Tuesday! Hooray!"

However a few days later he was still at the hospital. Every day he seemed dopier. I wondered if it was the new medication. No one seemed to help him get washed and dressed so usually when I arrived he was wandering around in pyjamas. Then I would help him to get washed and dressed unless I arrived in the evening. One day I brought in a colourful book full of recipes. He had so many of these back at the house and I thought he would like to look at the pictures. He smiled when we went through the book together. I talked to him about the different recipes remembering how he used to pick up new recipe books from the charity shops and try out different ones. His cooking had always been a very creative act, a mixture of a recipe from a book and his own ideas. Looking at the pictures of the food I suddenly started to feel sick so I left, looking back at him through the window as I went. He was still gazing at the book and still looking a bit dopey. I went home to bed with a bowl. I was very sick.

A few days later Bob was moved to the new dementia unit in Llangefni. It was much nicer. He had been very sick too, so they had decided to keep him in a bit longer. Maybe we both had had the same tummy bug. Hopefully, he would go back to Plas y Bryn very soon. I was allowed to take him out in the garden at the new unit. He walked so slowly and was quite wobbly. I held his hand as we walked. He seemed so very frail. He had always been so strong and now here I was holding his hand and propping him up, my poor darling man. I told myself off, yet again: I really had to face the possibility that he may not live much longer and I still had done nothing about funeral arrangements.

Perhaps he might live a few more years or perhaps he might die quite soon. There was no way I could be sure but I should be prepared. I told myself that I should make an appointment with the funeral directors and the Eternal Forest, the woodland burial place and choose a plot for us both. I knew what I should be doing but instead I went to the garden centre cafe and attempted to cheer myself up with an expensive lemon crunch and a cup of tea. Then I went to see Pete at the second hand furniture place he'd recently set up. It looked amazing. Then I went home for supper and fell asleep with my cat, Heidi, purring on my tummy.

Do you Remember?

Do you remember the wind in our hair?
The roar of the falls below, as we fled fast,
crags high above, down into the golden trees,
the dancing yellow leaves flying past,
on and on to the falls where we stopped
to drink the water's white foam, raw power
like our love, your strong arms around my waist
pouring all your roaring passion.

So do you remember now
as you sleep
or will you sleep through to that box
that too soon might hold you?
Dreaming of mountain tops,
dreaming of freedom,
your singing rising up and up
racing like the horses of your passion.

In the past, Bob used to always wear jeans, an old woollen sweater and a pair of walking boots. He always had several pairs of jeans in various states of repair. He very rarely wore anything smart. When he went to live at Plas y Bryn he took the few clothes he had with him apart from a spare pair of trousers that I kept in the house in case he had an accident when he came to visit me. More recently though I had bought him jogging bottoms with elastic in the waist as it made it easier for him and the carers to take them off and put them on. At first it had seemed odd to see him in these lose jogging bottoms. It felt like yet another loss of identity but then I became accustomed to this new identity. Before Bob went back to Plas y Bryn this time, I had to go out and buy some new, smaller jogging bottoms for him. He had lost so much weight and the old ones were in danger of falling down.

It was the beginning of November and at long last Bob was back at Plas y Bryn but it took him a week or more to settle and his behaviour was sometimes very erratic. One day I was very upset as the people at the home were complaining about Bob being difficult. One carer went on and on about it and I suppose I was afraid he might have to go back to the dementia unit again and I burst into tears. Bobby put his arms around me and held me while I sobbed and apologised for sobbing. He said, "No, it's good. Just let it all out." This made me sob even more. It was the longest sentence I'd heard him speak in a while.

I told him "Please be good, Bobby", but I don't think that meant anything to him. He just smiled and carried on holding me for a bit.

***

After a couple of weeks, Bob's behaviour was much better. He was sitting down to eat and he was sleeping well. His health seemed so much better too and I ceased to worry that he might die any time soon.

Frieda had invited me to come on a free holiday with her and Ray to Tunisia. It would be over Christmas and New Year and I would be helping her look after Ray who had Huntington's disease. I told her I would think about it. We would be away for about ten days.

Meanwhile, I was back to our old routine of days out to walk by the beach and days out at home and visiting friends: Gillian and Holger and others. We started going to the Talysarn market on a Friday. Bob loved it. We'd potter around the stalls and meet old neighbours and have a cup of tea and a cake. He always remembered people, though he could not manage more than "Hello" and sometimes, "How are you?"

One day in December, a particularly blowy day, we went down to Dinas Dinlle as we often did. The sun was low and streaming through the clouds over the sea, looking like some scene in an old oil painting of heaven. When we turned around there was a beautiful rainbow over the mountains. Bob was so happy to see all this, but the wind was getting stronger, nearly blowing him over, so fairly soon I packed him back in the car and we went off to Gillian's house for tea and carol singing. My darling man was so glad to be there. He ate cake with 'gusto' and then hummed away to all the carols. Sometimes he managed a few of the words. In 'Oh Come All Ye Faithful' he managed most of the chorus and hummed the rest. He was a happy man. Later, I took him back to the home and even then he was very happy and tucked into fish fingers, peas and chips with enthusiasm.

I decided I would go to Tunisia over Christmas now that Bob seemed calmer and more settled mentally and physically. I couldn't afford a holiday but Frieda would be paying in return for my help with Ray's care. It would be more of a holiday for her. I was very short of money so I was grateful for this working holiday but I also knew I needed to get a lot more chiropody work again to keep the wolf from the door.

On 23rd December Frieda, Ray and I left at midnight. I'd been over to see Bob nearly every day and he seemed happy and had put on a little weight again. He ate well, and the meals at the home were generally very good, but most people with dementia lose weight. Apparently as the brain struggles to survive the onslaught of the dementia, it uses up a lot of energy in the process. So Bob was still very thin and a bit wobbly. I gave him his cards and presents and Pete said he would pop in to see him. I explained to Bob that I would be back just after the New Year but I'm not sure whether he understood.

I had a lovely relaxing break away with Frieda and Ray. Looking after Ray was so easy compared with looking after Bob, and I also had a day away from the hotel and rode on a camel across the desert. We returned at the beginning of January. Snow and ice covered Great Britain; even the far end of Cornwall and the temperature in some parts was the lowest it had been for twenty years. The plane only just managed to land in Manchester. Most other airports were closed. It was difficult getting Ray in his wheelchair to Frieda's van, but we managed it after a struggle. The main roads were not too bad but many of the smaller ones were only just about passable. Plas y Bryn was difficult to reach as the narrow road had not been salted so it was several days before I was able to drive up there and bring Bob back the house. The care staff at Plas y Bryn said he'd been fine while I was away.

"Did you miss me?" I asked as we sat by the fire in my sitting room.

"Not at all", he answered.

As we were leaving, he slipped on the snow and I couldn't get him up. He was still quite heavy despite being skinny. I tried this way and that way but luckily my neighbour came to the rescue. We took an arm each and hauled him to his feet and then we both helped him to the car together. He didn't seem at all fazed by falling but I decided to wait until the snow had gone before I brought him home again.

At the end of January we visited the Talysarn market once more and afterwards we had a walk to the bench above the lake, just past the football pitch. There was still a lot of snow on Snowdon but it had mostly gone from the Nantlle ridge. The sun was low and the white cap of Snowdon was starting to turn pink. It was a beautiful evening. I said to Bob, "Look at Snowdon, isn't it beautiful!" Bob gazed up at the mountain. "It's magnificent!" he said.

Finding the Words.

There is some understanding still
behind the vacant sounds you make.
Your words, they have not flown,
migrated like a flock of birds,
but are locked up,
not like a dandelion clock
whose seeds have blown.

You are a burning ember, almost out,
until a sudden beauty makes you spark
and you rekindle magic words,
and you are heard like yesterday
when seeing Snowdon white with snow.
You said, "It is magnificent."
And hot with joy despite the cold,
I said, "Yes, yes, it is magnificent."

Bob's condition remained stable for quite a few months. I ceased to worry that he was about to die. He loved our trips out and was always happy to see me even when the weather was too foul to go anywhere much. He constantly mislaid his teeth, but he was getting better at 'gumming' his way through his food so he ate quite well. The carers said that he slept fairly well too.

Meanwhile, I was gradually building up more chiropody work which was a help to my finances, so I felt a lot happier. I was also busy with the final year of my M.A. and had joined a local walking group.

One particularly memorable afternoon, which started off in tipping rain, we went to the garden centre for a cup of tea. I bought Bob a cyclamen for his room and then the weather cleared up so we drove down to the Foryd, a stretch of flat land close to the Menai Straits and there we saw such wonderful sights. There were so many birds: oystercatchers, terns, whimbrels and curlews on the shore and then on the other side of the track a whole flock of lapwings took off as we walked past, their bodies glistening like jewels in the low light of the setting sun. It was all so beautiful. Bobby was exclaiming at the sights and then singing his heart out with happiness as we walked along. I was dancing over the large puddles to keep warm. I should have put warmer clothes on, but soon we were back at the car, both feeling so lighthearted, and listened to Bob's 'Caruso and the Legendary Tenors' CD all the way back to Plas y Bryn.

Back at the home, we sat in the car a while longer listening to the music but soon it was time for Bob's evening meal, so we went in. The staff were busy as usual but they were never too busy to say a friendly hello and smile. The little dogs that belonged to the boss came trotting down the corridor and as we crossed the garden to Bob's section someone was shutting the hens up for the night and called out as we passed, "Hello, Bob. Have you had a nice afternoon?"

Bob so wanted to tell everyone about the flocks of birds but his words were just gobbledygook. The carer and I nodded and looked as if we understood, and I interjected with just enough real words so that he could reply to Bob's enthusiastic sounds:

"Wow! That's amazing, Bob."

Inside, supper was being served. I stayed to help. Mary was there as she was in charge of Bob's section, and Ken, one of the residents who was often bad tempered, suddenly shouted at her.

"Oh Jesus Christ!"

"No, only Mary," said Mary.

During late winter and early spring I went to Cornwall a couple of times but apart from that I was very busy with chiropody work, finishing off my M.A., growing vegetables in my garden and taking Bob out regularly.

***

In May my sister, Jenny, came to stay for a week with her dog, Guinness. She'd not seen Bob for years and had never been to North Wales. It was lovely weather so we had a wonderful time swimming in the local lakes and walking on the mountains, not big walks as she was struggling with arthritis in her back and in her ankle. I introduced her to some of my friends and neighbours.

I was nervous of her meeting Bob again with him being so changed.

When I went to fetch him, he was being very difficult. I thought at first that he was picking up on my nervousness, but it was just that he'd done a poo in his nappy pants. Once we'd got that sorted out he was fine. Jenny was lovely with him and we had tea in the garden and went for a little walk up the lane with Guinness, the dog.

Coming back from our walk we had to leave Bob standing by the recycling plastic boxes at the front door while we went to get the key which I'd hidden in the back porch (I was in the habit of hiding keys when Bob was around otherwise he would pick them up and hide them somewhere). When we came back half a minute later, Bob was sitting inside one of the recycling boxes and his bum was completely stuck. We lifted him up, blue bin and all and then had to prise the bin off his bottom. We stood there, all three of us, giggling our heads off.

***

After Jenny's visit, time seemed to fly by. Suddenly, or so it seemed, it was Bob's birthday. It was a lovely morning so I took Bob to one of his favourite valleys, Cwm Pennant. We stopped at the first bridge as the land was flatter there and then we walked along beside the river. The grasshoppers were making their own type of music, rubbing their back legs together, a jutting, tutting sound; the birds were singing; the sheep were bleating and the river joined in with its own gentle melody. Bob looked so content, ambling through the long grass. After a while, we stopped on the river bank and I got out the picnic mat and our picnic.

It was warm and Bob happily lay back, sleepy in the sunshine while I broke up a pork pie (his favourite) and fed it to him in small pieces so he could gum his way through it - he had lost his teeth again. After our lunch, we walked back across the fields, amongst the sheep and the thistles, and drove back to Plas y Bryn for tea. They usually made a cake for the residents when it was their birthday but somehow the cook had forgotten. I think he then made one in a hurry and when it finally arrived it was not the best.

Anyway, by then Bob was restless and marched up and down the corridor, cake in one hand, a glass of wine in other, spilling it as he went. I trailed after him trying to persuade him to come and sit down, to no avail so I decided it was time I went. He hardly registered me going. I had a quick swim in the lake and then prepared a meal for some friends of mine who were coming to stay. Finally, I sat down to eat and chat and relax in their welcome company.

On July 10th I wrote:

"Eight years ago tonight, Bob and I first slept in this house, in this bed. I remember that Bob started in the night at the sound of a gate. It was actually our neighbour's gate, but it sounded just like ours. Bob was always easily woken by unexpected sounds. I remember lying beside Bob, almost too excited to sleep. I remember thinking as I lay there that here we were in Wales, starting a new life together! I remember imagining that we would live the

rest of our lives together here in this place, together forever or at least until we were ninety or more! How little we know of the future... Tonight I sit in bed alone and listen to the rain and the sound of my little cat Heidi washing herself on the other side of the bed."

***

The next day I collected my M.A. from Bangor University. I was very nervous but it all went well, and it was lovely to see my friends from the course. I was almost the last to be called up onto the stage and I was terrified that I'd trip on the stairs or shake the wrong hand or that my mortar board would fall off but it all went fine and we had a jolly buffet lunch afterwards. I suppose I might have felt sad that Bob could not share this moment with me but I tried not to think about what *might* have been. It was my coping mechanism to put such feelings in a box and shut the door. As I had started the course when Bob already had dementia it had always felt like a time to escape from looking after him, a time to spend with other human beings who didn't have dementia. It was something I really enjoyed and had succeeded at, despite Bob, and I thought to myself after the ceremony that I should pat myself on the back that I had actually got through the course despite everything else.

Obviously, if Bob had not been ill with dementia he would have been very proud of me and would have encouraged me to do my best but I could not think about how things *might have been* without feeling a great deal of pain.

So while I was at the ceremony I put Bob in one box and then I went home and closed that box and opened the Bob box. I got changed into more normal clothes and took Bob out for a short walk by the sea and an ice cream.

***

It was the end of July and Bob was being more difficult again and having more violent mood swings. One day he was having one of his mood swings and head-butted one of his favourite carers and broke her nose. The poor woman had to have time off work and when she returned she told him:

"I know you didn't mean to Bob, but you broke my nose."

"Oh, I'm so sorry." He looked sorry too.

The trouble was that when he got into one of his agitated angry states he didn't seem to be aware of what he was doing and things got broken. However, as far as I know, this was the first time he'd ever actually really hurt someone.

***

It was the beginning of August and Kira and Angel and the two girls came to stay with me. (Jasper was being looked after by his other grandparents). They had decided to move to Wales and were looking for a place to rent.

One day when Kira and Angel had gone off house hunting, I spent the day looking after Rosy and Amber. When I asked them what they would like to do, they said that they wanted to see Bobby.

As Bob had been more difficult again recently, it was with a little trepidation that I brought him back home for the afternoon but I need not have worried. The two girls were wonderful with their Bobby. He was especially happy to see Amber, who he adored, and they gave each other a big hug. Rosy was a bit more reserved. The girls had been baking cupcakes so Amber got them out and gave Bob the little cake that she'd especially decorated for him and he had it with his cup of tea. We then went in the car to the play park. Bob sat on the bench while the girls played on the swings and the slide. After a while I thought he might be getting cold as it was quite breezy.

"Shall we go down to the river?" I suggested. So we went for a short walk to the river. The girls held Bob's hands and helped him not to wobble too much on the rough grass and then, when we reached the bridge, Amber said, "Let's play Pooh sticks". So we did. The girls scrabbled around in the trees and bushes and soon had quite a selection of sticks.

"Here you are Bobby", said Amber, "now lean over the bridge and we'll all drop our sticks in together. One two, three, go!"

Somehow Amber knew that she had to show Bob how to do things, as if he was younger than her. It was a magical time of laughter and fun.

"Whey hey!" shouted Bob as he threw his stick in the air.

"Don't throw your stick Bobby", said Amber, "just drop it in."

"Oh yes", said Bob and giggled.

Then it was time to take him back. He was getting very tired and could only just manage to walk up the slight slope to the car. Back at Plas y Bryn, the girls helped him up the steps; one on either side, and once inside, they both gave him a hug goodbye. Their loving acceptance of Bob and his dementia brought tears to my eyes.

***

Around this time I came into a sum of money so I decided to go back to my favourite country, Nepal for about three weeks in September. My friend Geoff was going with a group of friends and someone had dropped out so I was invited to take their place. It was too good an opportunity to miss. I agonized about leaving the country and Bob, but his health seemed quite stable and Pete and Gillian and Holger said they would look out for him. Gillian's father, Jim was now in Plas y Bryn as well. In fact, he was in the same section as Bob so they could visit both men at the same time.

Kira and Angel were still house hunting in North Wales, so far without success, so they were going to stay in my house and look after Heidi, and the hens. The day before I left for Nepal the children insisted I should have an early birthday and they baked me a cake.

"Have you any birthday candles, Granny?" I never throw anything away – so I found a box of birthday candle stubs and left them to it. Amber counted out sixty two and stuck them all over the cake. I wasn't allowed to see it so I didn't know. They invited a few neighbours around and then Amber came in with the cake! Wow! Talk about a fire hazard!

Anyway, I soon had them all blown out and then we had to skim the top of the cake off as it was a bit singed!

Afterwards I went to Plas y Bryn to see Bob and say goodbye to all the staff as well. Bob seemed very well. I gave him a great big hug. I thought to myself, "I do hope he will be okay..."

The next day I got on the train to Manchester and boarded the plane to Kathmandu. It was a wonderful trip but later, on refection, I think I should not have gone. When I returned, I was a bit tired and jet lagged but I went straight round to see Bob.

Apparently he had been very difficult while I was away and Dr Kurian had put him on a new drug. I was used to the fact that Bob's medication had to be changed from time to time and usually the change seemed to help Bob but this time it was not good. I went to see the nurse about it. I told her so. Bob was 'zombified' and he had swollen feet. I asked her what the drug was and she got the leaflet out of the box and gave it to me. She said she wasn't happy with him taking it either.

"But our hands are tied," she said.

***

Over the next couple of weeks or so, the bad side effects of the drug really began to kick in. Bob became more and more bent over and his feet more swollen. He was barely able to shuffle around and when I tried to take him out it was a complete nightmare. He was so confused and walking up and down any steps was almost impossible so we had to use the lift. When we got to the car he had great difficulty lifting his legs to get in and then he found it very difficult to climb out so in the end I felt unable to take him out at all. I was very frightened of what was happening to him and asked and asked that he be taken off the drug.

I wrote this poem about Bob and the drug that he was taking which was called Haloperidol.

Haloperidol

'Try this good old antipsychotic on him,

slow him down.

Stop him going AWOL.'

The packet says:

'You may have some side effects while you are taking

your capsules.'

You may

have Jaundice, sore throats, ulcers in your mouth.

It may

make you produce milk.

and affect your periods,

if you are a woman

and give you breasts

if you are a man.

It may

make you unable to have sex,

build up fluid in your body.

Or it may

turn your muscles rigid

change your face,

make you feverish, give you rashes

cause muscles to spasm in your neck and shoulders,

and make you gag.

Oh and the packet adds that there have been

'cases of sudden and unexplained death in patients but
it is not known whether the deaths were due to the
medicine.'

Well yes, that's good,

he's still alive.

'And look how well he's eating now he's sitting down.'

Never mind

he'll hardly walk, hardly get up.

He doesn't cause much trouble now.

Never mind

his drawn down face,

the rigid muscles of a man of five foot ten

who's now so bent he's five foot two.

Never mind

his only view's two rather swollen feet.

But it's okay, they'll say,

He's still alive.

Apparently Plas y Bryn was in a difficult situation because Dr Kurian, who was in charge of the drugs he took, was away on holiday and couldn't be contacted. The nurse said I could talk to Bob's GP but when he came to see Bob he was completely useless and more or less said that Bob was like he was because he was old. I was furious. I said I wanted a second opinion.

Another local GP visited Bob and finally he was taken off the medication but he was still so bent over and had withdrawn into himself. He kept trying to straighten up as the effects of the drug began to wear off and was forever leaning sideways and falling against doors and walls and bruising himself. I decided to write to Dr Kurian about the frightening effect that the drug had on Bob. I doubted that Bob would ever really recover from such horrible side effects but I told Dr Kurian that maybe he should "think not twice, but a hundred times before giving out such a drug to frail elderly people". I also sent Dr Kurian a copy the poem 'Haloperidol'.

Later, to Dr Kurian's credit, he did write back to me and apologised.

***

Alexis came to stay in early November to pick up a trailer load of stuff for her pottery business. A friend of a friend of mine was giving up being a potter and I was told that all his equipment was free to a good home. It was too good an opportunity for Alexis to miss. Another friend was lending me his trailer as mine was too small for pottery wheels and the like.

On November 10th Alexis and I were heading down to Cornwall with the trailer when Bob had a stroke. Pete was by his bedside and told me that it was not life threatening and that I shouldn't change my plans. However, I was feeling so upset I could hardly drive and kept wanting to turn around and go straight back to the hospital. The weather was terrible with rain and a howling gale. The tarpaulin I bought to cover the pottery stuff was getting ripped.

Alexis took over the driving: I was in no fit state to drive. Everything felt like some sort of nightmare. We kept stopping to tie the tarpaulin back into position but by the time we reached Penzance it was totally shredded and the wind and rain showed no sign of abating.

The journey had taken hours and it was nearly 11 o'clock at night. The next morning we drove to the pottery shed that Alexis was renting and got everything inside. Then I rang the hospital. Bobby was in Tryfan ward. They said that he was comfortable. I rang Pete.

"I want to come straight back Pete. I should be by Bob's bedside." But Pete told me not to be stupid.

"You're exhausted. It's horrible weather. You need to rest. There's nothing you can do, Ali. There's no point in you rushing back. He's not about to die."

Another of my friends, Jill, who I was staying with, said the same. "You need to rest!"

While I was there, I walked up onto the moor above Penzance and sat amongst the standing stones known as the 'Nine Maidens'.

I got out my diary and wrote that it all seemed so unreal. Bob was in hospital with tubes attached to him. It suddenly seemed that it was only yesterday we were here, walking across this very moor, before we ever went to Wales. He was singing an aria, while I danced around and clapped when he had finished. So many pictures of our short time together welled up and flooded my memory.

***

After a few days' rest, I drove straight to Bangor hospital. When I arrived at the ward his bed was curtained off and I had to wait while he was being washed and changed. Looking out of the window I could see his favourite mountains, the Carneddau. I felt the irony of such a view. The mountains he loved so near and yet so far. All I could hear him say behind the curtains was "sssss ddddd".

A few days later Bob was moved to a hospital in Holyhead, Ysbyty Penrhos Stanley, so I had a long way to go to see him. Apparently there had been complaints about Bob's care home and until these had been investigated he couldn't go back. I wondered if the people who complained realised how much trouble they were causing. Of course they didn't, but I now had a hundred mile round trip every time I wanted to see Bob. As far as I was concerned, I was very happy with the care they gave at Plas y Bryn and I just wanted him back there so I could get to see him easily.

***

On the following Sunday, Kira came with me to visit Bob and he seemed a lot better. He was sitting up a little and tried to kiss me in a very mouthy way. He couldn't talk at all and the nurses said he was having difficulty swallowing, so they were giving him a thick creamy substance to drink. I was very grateful for Kira's company. She gave me moral support as I was finding it difficult to come to terms with everything that had happened to Bob these last two weeks.

Also I was very tired and so she drove. On the way home, she took me to see the house that she and Angel were going to rent in Llangefni. It seemed very nice with plenty of room for everyone. It had certainly taken a long time for them to find a house and I hoped that this one wouldn't fall through as several others had done. I was looking forward to having my own place back. Much as I loved my family, I needed my own space.

A few days later I visited Bob on my own. Pete had given me some grapes for Bob. I wasn't sure he'd be able to eat them. He was having great difficulty swallowing solid food. I asked the nurses and they said the grapes might make him choke so not to feed them to him. I ate some of them myself. While I was there the specialist came to talk to me. He spoke quite bluntly about Bob, but in as kindly a way as he could. He said that there was little chance of recovery and that because of the dementia he would probably just continue to deteriorate. I said I quite understood and I was then quite honest and blunt too.

I said that I just hoped Bob wouldn't live too much longer. Really, I felt that if he could not eat properly, could not walk and could no longer speak, what was left? He could have no quality of life. I thought to myself that if he was a dog, the vet would be suggesting we put him down. I felt numb inside, unable to really think straight or contact my feelings. After that day I just took each day, one day at a time. I decided to do what I could to make what Bob had left to him as good as possible, so I went out and bought a new CD player, a really nice one with a good tone and asked the nurses if they wouldn't mind him listening to it. Music was something he could still enjoy and it would lift his spirits.

Time went on and Bob was still at the hospital. He was still giving me very mouthy kisses. I knew it was his only way of telling me he loved me, but it felt very odd. His mouth didn't feel like Bob's mouth anymore, poor love. He should have gone back at Plas y Bryn on the Friday but there was so much snow and ice on the roads, they had deemed it necessary to wait. Then they seemed to be dragging their feet again. No one seemed to know what was holding things up so I went to see the head nurse in Bob's ward to ask what was going on. She said that she didn't understand the email that Plas y Bryn had sent her so I persuaded her to phone them for clarification.

"Here is their phone number." I said "Maybe you could phone them, please".

Soon after this phone call, Bob went back to Plas y Bryn and around about the same time Kira and family moved to their new home in Llangefni. It was a lovely house and their landlady seemed very nice.

***

I called in to see Bob the day they moved out to Llangefni. One of the carers was with him in his room playing him his favourite music. He had a special bed now, with cot sides, so he couldn't fall out. It was a waterbed which would hopefully stop him getting bedsores. Bob was falling asleep so I didn't stay long. I didn't feel like going home straight away, so I called in to see Gillian. She made me a cup of tea and we sat and talked. She told me that her father, Jim, was fading fast. He had been at Plas Y Bryn about as long as Bob and had been getting slowly worse and worse. Gillian and I hugged each other. I hoped I could be there for her as she had been there for me. She had always been someone I could turn too in the good times and the bad. Afterwards I went home to bed and I thought to myself as I fell asleep, "I shall miss the family being here but I shan't miss their mess".

***

A few days later Jim died and I went with Gillian, Holger, and Dafydd in their car to his funeral at the crematorium in Bangor. There was some snow around and more was forecast. I went up to Plas y Bryn after the funeral. They had got Bob up and he was in a wheelchair. He gave me a sloppy kiss and smiled.

A day or so later snow fell and then overnight even more fell. I had parked my car in the car park in Talysarn when I heard the forecast but I was not going to go anywhere in a car and cancelled my chiropody appointments. I put on my wellies and I called in on the neighbours to see if they needed anything. One asked for a newspaper and another for a bottle of milk. Then I walked across the fields and over the bridge and along the lane to Penygroes. There were no cars on the road. The only sound was the crunch of snow under my feet. On the way I met two little children being pulled along on a sledge by a father who couldn't get to work.

When I got to the Co-op it looked as if there'd been a herd of locusts in the shop: panic buying had hit Penygroes! All the bread and potatoes had gone but I did manage to get the milk and newspaper for my neighbours and a few bits for myself and walked home. Everything looked so beautiful under its white blanket but it meant I couldn't get up to see Bob until the 22nd of December and even then I had to walk some of the way. The road was too icy and there was still so much snow on the ground but I was determined to get there for Bob had had another slight stroke and was semi-conscious. I felt so upset to see him like that. I wrote:

"There's never a convenient time to die, but please, Bobby, hang on in there a bit. It's Christmas my dear love. But then, what will be, will be."

Bob's last Christmas

By Christmas Eve a lot of the snow had melted and amazingly Bob was so much better. It was like a miracle. One day I thought he was going to die and two days later he was sitting up in his wheelchair and trying to eat.

On Christmas Eve, I went over to my family. I cooked a chicken for them and took all my presents and some mail for them. Rosy had a new pet for Christmas. It was a hamster called Peanut. She was a lively little creature. They hadn't got much furniture yet so we all sat on the floor to open our presents while Peanut rolled around us in his 'Hamster Ball'.

I had Christmas lunch at Plas y Bryn with Bob. He was up and dressed and in his wheelchair. We all wore party hats. The home had laid on a feast and Bob did his best to eat his Christmas dinner. They had to mash and mince it up but he still enjoyed it and gave me another sloppy kiss. He looked so very frail and tired after the meal and the staff said they were going to help him back to bed very soon, so I left and went for a walk, very grateful for this day, this hour, this minute. It was cold, but dry and I watched the sun go down and then went to visit a neighbour who was bedridden before returning home to my cat, a warm fire and a bit of television before going to bed.

I had another lovely Christmas dinner with Gillian and Holger on the 27th and then Amber and Rosy came over to stay with me for a few days. Their father, Ariel, came up to see them. He only stayed for two days. Amber and Rosy were upset by him not staying longer and after he'd gone they both insisted that they wanted to see their Bobby. Against my better judgement, I said they could, though I warned them they might be upset to see him so thin and ill. They hadn't seen him since the summer. Poor Amber was terribly upset.

"Granny, why are his legs so thin?" she cried.

She fled from the home as quickly as she could. Rosy took her upset out on the hens in the garden and chased them around until I arrived to stop her. I took them to the fun centre in Caernarfon after that and chased around with them in the ballpark for an hour or so. Hopefully that helped them to feel a lot happier. I decided I wouldn't take them to see Bob again, it was just too painful.

***

Little by little, Bob shrank. He had good days and then other days when he slept a lot. He was finding it harder to swallow again and often had some of the specially fortified milky cream mixture to boost his energy. Over and over again I asked the home could they please keep him there, even with him so weak.

"I don't want him sent back to the hospital. Please let him die in peace here." I said.

"He's happy here." They said they would do their best.

***

Towards the end of January, I went to an enquiry with the manager of Plas Y Bryn. It was an enquiry into how Bob had acquired bruises on his sides before he went into hospital with the bad stroke. There were lots of very official people at the enquiry and they gave the manager a lot of stick. She was told that her staff needed more training and that they needed to keep better records.

I put my oar in then. I told them how Bob's spine became very bent because of the side effects of the medicine, haloperidol.

I told how concerned the staff at the home were and how once he was taken off the medication he kept falling sideways against doors and walls when he was trying to straighten himself up and walk properly again and that that was why he had those bruises.

I spoke of my appreciation of the real care given by the staff at the home and added that if they had to spend half their time writing records, they wouldn't have time to give such good care.

I left feeling old and out of step and just grateful that I didn't work for the NHS with this blame and claim culture.

I was never told the results of the inquiry, but as nothing dreadful happened (i.e. Bob was not sent somewhere else) I presumed that the staff at Plas Y Bryn were not blamed for Bob's bruises. To be honest I did not ask. Bob was dying; I just wanted him left in peace to die and to stay in the place he knew where he would be looked after by people who knew him.

***

I sometimes felt as if I was standing on the edge of a precipice looking down into an abyss. I was trying to be as prepared as I could be for Bob's death. I had organised everything. He had a will and a funeral plan now, with the local funeral directors, and I had bought a burial plot at the Eternal Forest. But I could not organise my heart. I could not imagine life without him even though there was so little of him left. His body was shrinking and becoming more twisted, but at least I could still hold his hand and stroke his arm and kiss his cheek. I could still sit by his bedside and play him his favourite music and I could still talk to him even though he could not answer me. I could not think about it too much. When I wasn't visiting Bob I kept myself very busy with work and walking. One day I took Kira and Amber and Rosy to the woodland burial place, the Eternal Forest, and showed them where the plot was that I'd chosen for Bob. It was a double plot so I could be buried there too, eventually.

Bob had good days when they would get him into his wheelchair and bad days when he would just sleep. Whenever I could, I would arrive at meal times so I could help to feed him. Usually he could only manage some thick soup and some specially thickened tea. Anything too solid or too liquid would usually make him choke.

***

At the beginning of February, when I was busy at work with lots of people's feet to do, the home phoned me to say, "Would you come in please, Bob is very ill. His blood pressure has dropped dramatically". I rushed over there and sat by his bedside. Later, he rallied, woke up and ate some soup. I spoke to the nurse reiterating what I had said to her before.

"Please don't have Bob carted off to hospital unnecessarily trying to prolong his life, not unless he's in terrible pain and you don't have the expertise to deal with it here. He's happy here."

A few days later Bob was suddenly so much better again. He was sitting up in his wheelchair and trying to hum a tune, bless him.

On February 14th I took Bob a pot full of miniature daffodils for Valentine's Day. His face lit up at the sight of them. He always loved flowers. He touched the petals gently with his finger tips and stuttered out a few sounds and then smiled as best he could. I smiled back and nodded and looked into his eyes. Somehow we communicated wordlessly. I felt he was trying to communicate his love of beauty. He must have so missed going out into the countryside and seeing the flowers and the trees and the mountains. I really missed taking him.

A few days later I was in bed with a tummy bug so I didn't go to see Bob until I was better. I got down my book of Gerard Manley Hopkins poems and decided to write one of my own.

***

Towards the end of March I went to London to be with my sister, Jenny, for a couple of days. She was having a foot operation and there was no one else to help look after her. Her daughter, Sarah, was coming over from Italy as soon as she could. Frieda asked,

"What will you do if Bob dies while you are away?"

"Well, I'll just have to hope he doesn't." I said in a rather matter of fact way when I didn't feel like that at all. I was glad to help my sister but I was relieved to get home again and hurry to his bedside and hold his hand. He was still with us. His body was shrinking more and more and becoming very twisted and stiff so that it was very difficult for the staff to wash him and dress him without him moaning. They tried to be as careful as they could but as time went on every movement caused him more and more discomfort. Time seemed to slow to one day, one hour, and one minute at a time. I came in every day but I could do little more

I Take No Veil

Inspired by Gerard Manley Hopkins

I have been where storms sway
the seas swell green and grey.
There was no haven: hell or beauty.

I have lain in warm haystacks,
on sharp rocks, in ruined shacks
watching the wax and wane.

And where ravens rise and fall
in the lashing rain and the wind,
I have climbed high until I crawled.

But seeing your eyes, your vacant face,
your voice now lost in tumbling,
I leave the hills to find that place
where *you* are my field of beauty.

than hold his hand. There was one day when he did sit up for a little while. He tried to sing a tune, but he only managed a few notes. I wrote a poem about that moment.

Running Down the Hill

Two days before you died you sang five notes
out of clear blue song.
I wanted to say 'Go on, go on,'
but the moment sighed and passed,
and outside the sunlight tilted sideways on a tall ash tree.
I had looked away
and I thought of your mother waiting for you at the gate
and you
a child again,
Running.

And another day I wrote this poem, sitting by his bedside while he slept:

Spin Dreaming

Amongst the trees in windswept air
you dream of walking, breathing deeply,
strength refilling lungs to sing
your favourite Aria, loud and clear.

Locked in this contorted frame
far away you are spin-dreaming,
no more anger, no more blame,
this last of you is spiralling.

Your carers, trying to ease your pain,
don't feel the gusts of freedom's hurricane,
or hear your song in stream's cascading.
They simply stop to check you're breathing.

On April 6th my dearest love, my Bobby died about 8:30 in the morning. I went straight to Plas y Bryn when they rang. They'd said he was still alive but he had gone before I got to the home.

He looked very peaceful. I sat beside him and kissed his cheek and, feeling that his spirit was still in the room, I played some of his favourite music. I would have liked to have sat there peacefully beside him for a while but the nurse kept coming in, even though I had asked her if I could have some time alone with him. Then a young police woman came to look at him and fill in a form. Apparently it was 'standard procedure'.

I then went to see the manager of the home and filled in further forms and then I went to see the undertakers. Kira said she would phone everyone for me to tell them he had died. I was very grateful to her. I couldn't face that job. Deb and Andy said they would tell all our friends and neighbours in our little hamlet.

"Everyone is welcome to his funeral, tell them", I said to Deb, "when I have a date".

I then took their dog Jazz for a long walk. I felt Bob was there too, walking beside me. He loved Jazz.

Later, I went to pick up the death certificate and called into Gillian's for a cup of tea.

Sometime during the evening I realised I had forgotten to eat all day. I went to sleep sending my love to Bob's spirit. As soon as I closed my eyes I found myself remembering him as he had been when I first knew him. I imagined him holding my hand and eventually I fell asleep.

***

A few days later I went to see Bob at the funeral parlour. They had done a magnificent job. He looked so tall and straight, very grave and calm.

"You look magnificent in your cream satin, my dearest." I touched his cheek and kissed him. So cold it felt on my lips.

***

On 14th April we buried Bob in the woodland of the Eternal Forest. It was a cloudy day, though the sun did break through briefly. I got up early and picked some flowers in the garden to make a spray to go on his coffin. Then I gathered petals and leaves for us to sprinkle into his grave. Everything went well and everyone was so kind and loving. His coffin was pushed up the track to the grave side on a lovely wooden wagon. Neighbours lent a bit of muscle to the undertaker's efforts. I played his favourite music on a portable CD player. I said a few simple words. I was quite choked up when I started to speak. My friend Carol read a poem.

We had a short time of silence when people were able to speak if they felt moved to do so, like in a Quaker meeting. I remember Dafydd spoke about their shared love of motorbikes. I read the poem I wrote just before he died.

After that the undertakers lowered his coffin into the grave and we all sprinkled petals onto him. Then I gave out a few spades and while some filled the grave in, others danced around to Enya's song 'How can I keep from singing'. Afterwards, those who could spare the time came back to the Nantlle valley for a cup of tea and cake. Then I went home and sat for a long while. I think I ate a little and then I wrote about Bob's funeral in my diary finishing with: "It is late now and I think I shall go to bed."

***

For a long, long time after I felt very empty. But strangely, I found that the Bob I remembered was not the painfully thin man who had had dementia and could no longer walk or speak. It was as if some large whale had swum into my brain and swallowed that person up in one gulp. The Bob I remembered was striding over the mountains of Wales and along the coasts of Cornwall. He was the tall and strong man who had flashing blue eyes and jutting eyebrows and he would sing beautifully and powerfully as he walked and often there were times when he would talk and talk until you were talked into the ground and I would say:

"Bobby, would you mind if we walked in silence for a bit."

He was the man that held me in his arms, a passionate lover but as stubborn as they come. He had no 'side' to him. What you saw was what he was. A free spirit who would not be tamed, he was sometimes too honest for his own good, but generally polite, friendly and kind to everyone he met. He was the man who held doors open for me, who would come back home after we'd had words, his eyes flashing with a bunch of flowers for me protruding from his jacket and I would feel weak at the knees.

Often I felt that he was like Pooh Bear and I was like Piglet, friends laughing and playing together, forever and forever!

I still hear his voice when I cross a busy road:

"Give us your paw" he'd say.

Acknowledgements

I firstly want to thank the members of the Disability Arts Cymru English Writers group. They gave me the courage to keep writing when I was ready to throw the towel in.

Secondly I want to thank my publishers Dafydd Monks and Jessika Thiele of Herbary Books for all their help from designing the book cover, the final editing, to publicising and publishing.

Thirdly and most of all I want to thank Eabhan Ni Shuileabhain for editing the several editions of the manuscript and for the solid advice and encouragement she gave me.

WITH A LOVE FOR BOOKS

With a large range of imprints, from herbalism, self-sufficiency, physical and mental wellbeing, food, memoirs and many more, Herbary Books is shaped by the passion for writing and bringing innovative ideas close to our readers.

All our authors put their hearts into their books and as publishers we just lend a helping hand to bring their creation to life.

Thank you to our authors and to you, dear reader.

Discover and purchase all our books on

WWW.HERBARYBOOKS.COM

HERBARY BOOKS

CPSIA information can be obtained
at www.ICGtesting.com
Printed in the USA
LVHW011754201220
674691LV00014B/1694